WOODHE

---- PART TWO ----
DUNFORD BRIDGE, PENISTONE,
SHEFFIELD VICTORIA
and via the Worsborough Branch to Wath

An 04 emerges from the smoking Hades of Woodhead Tunnel with an Up freight train composed, largely, of empty wagons and heads into Dunford Bridge station which lay directly ahead. The Robinson 2-8-0, arguably the best freight engine ever built, and the tunnel itself epitomised the railway that was universally known as "The Woodhead Line". *H. Gordon Tidey*

E.M.JOHNSON

Copyright © E M Johnson and Foxline Publishing

ISBN 1 870119 52 5

All rights reserved

Typesetting, Layout, Design & Maps/Diagrams
  by Gregory Fox

Printed by the Amadeus Press, Huddersfield

Published by Foxline Publishing

32 Urwick Road Romiley Stockport SK6 3JS

Foreword

The first volume of Woodhead appears to have been very well received. What emerges clearly is the tremendous, almost magnetic, attraction that the line seems to have held for both enthusiast and railwayman alike. My approach of looking at the broader aspects of the railway and concentrating largely on the pre - Electric era seems to have gone down well. The inclusion of the section dealing with the OA&GB and that part of the Stalybridge branch as far as Dukinfield seemed to be popular, although one critic took me to task for not going to Stalybridge itself!

Since the first drafts were made for part one, a great deal of historical information dealing with the MSW electrification has been discovered. I had already researched extensively the electrification project ready for this volume, but as a consequence it has now been decided to leave aside almost completely the MSW project and to direct the greater part of this towards a third volume.

Now, with the smokey confines of Woodhead behind us, we can concentrate on the run down towards Sheffield Victoria and take in en route one or two interesting deviations.

Woodhead Reservoir, c.1920: In the Longdendale Valley, broadly between Hadfield and Woodhead itself, runs a succession of reservoirs - vast stretches of man - made lakes laid down by the Victorians for the benefit of the citizens of Manchester. What this stretch of railway looked like before the reservoirs came we cannot show; what we can provide is this magnificent study by a man once described as "one of the fathers of railway photography," H. Gordon Tidey. He began photographing trains in the 1890's and claimed to devote one whole week each year entirely to railway photography. Certainly, his few shots on the Woodhead line are amongst the very best taken on this remarkable railway. Our view is set alongside Woodhead reservoir, completed in the 1870's by the esteemed water engineer John Frederick Bateman. Looking west towards Crowden, two Robinson 8K 2-8-0's are engaged in moving Woodhead's lifeblood - coal traffic. The engine on the Up Goods (loop line) is moving about 45 - 50 empty coal wagons back to the Yorkshire pits and is approaching milepost 18; its companion on the Down Main moves in excess of 22 loaded wagons downhill towards Crowden station, just out of sight around the far bend. Development of the railway here was in two phases: the main line had opened from Dinting to Woodhead on August 8th. 1844. An MS&L line plan drawn up and originally dated 1884 shows the land jutting out into the reservoir as having been sold to Manchester Corporation on September 21st 1866. Calculated at ARP (Acres, Roods and Poles) 1-1-½, it was owned by Lord Edward G. F. Howard, Duke of Norfolk. Marked on the plan as "For Widening", it was not until over forty years later that the plans bore fruit. The Goods lines, usually referred to as "Loops", were brought into use between Crowden and Woodhead in 1908; the Up Goods on August 24th, the Down on October 5th.   *H. Gordon Tidey*

By Torside Reservoir, 1920's: Class B3 4-6-0 No. **6165**, *Valour*-once the pride of Gorton shed, runs down the 1-in-117 from Crowden past milepost 16¼ towards Torside with a 5-coach Marylebone to Manchester Express; a horsebox has been attached to the rear of the train. This lovely Summer scene shows at a glance the wild and rugged beauty of the Longdendale Valley. The main lines are flanked on either side by loops, properly referred to as "Goods Lines". Dating from 1907, these greatly aided the movement of the vast amount of slow-moving coal traffic which was the life-blood of this railway. In the background is the eastern end of Torside Reservoir-one of a series constructed by Manchester Corporation between 1854 and 1877 to provide water for their city.

H. Gordon Tidey

Contents

Dedication

I would like to dedicate this second part of "Woodhead" to my dear Parents in Law, Frank and Kathleen Abell, who both passed away while this book was in the making.

Between Valehouse and Torside, 1945: Now for something completely different! As a change from all those wonderful Robinson Class O4s-here is another LNER 2-8-0, No **8532**. However, before my readers reach for their pens to correct me, this was an LNER engine albeit one on loan, and built by the LNER. No 8532 was one of a batch of ten engines built at Doncaster in 1945 to the standard LMS Stanier design; the type having been adopted by the War Department as the WD standard goods engine towards the end of 1939. Some of these "foreigners" (but not this one) were given the LNER classification O6 before being returned, eventually, to their parent company. In the case of No 8532, she was dispatched to the LMS in March 1947. Here, this fine Stanier engine heads along the Down Goods line between Torside and Valehouse with a train of loaded coke wagons-notice the high sides necessary to accommodate this bulky fuel.
Collection of Ted Hancock

Acknowledgments

Preparation of this volume has extended over the last two and a half years and help in its writing has come from many different individuals and sources. First I must acknowledge the kindness, patience and support of my dear wife, Mary, who has provided me with unstinting help and assistance through what has been a most trying and difficult time for her. Secondly, to Greg Fox, my publisher, in accommodating all my various demands and alterations over the time it has taken me to write this book. Also, my thanks to him for producing the maps and for helping me to locate much valuable source material. To Howard Turner and Ted Hancock, I acknowledge sincere thanks for imparting their unsurpassed knowledge of Sheffield's transport system to me and for helping me with many gems from their respective collections. On my frequent visits to Sheffield, Howard and Ted have been my "native guides" and, but for them, I don't think I could have navigated my way very far beyond Dunford Bridge! Benny McVey shared with me his many reminiscences of that remote spot as well as providing me with much useful information and help with many photographs and points of railway operation. Sincere thanks as well to Allan Brown for allowing me access to his researches covering Neepsend shed and to his photographic collection; to my good friends Brian Green, Doug Darby and Ronnie Gee for allowing me access to their superb negatives which have yielded some of the finest pictures ever taken on this wonderful railway. Ken Boulter and Peter Hughes have, too, helped greatly with splendid photographic coverage from earlier years. John Quick has been of much assistance with details round the Deepcar and Oughty Bridge districts and David Green and Ron Fareham have done likewise with their unrivalled knowledge of the Penistone, Barnsley and Wath areas.

Sincere thanks are offered also to the following people who have all helped with photographic material or information in one way or another: Gordon Biddle, Rod Blencowe, Jack Braithwaite, Ben Brooksbank, Roger Carpenter, Richard Casserley, B.N.Collins, Gordon Coltas, the late Jim Davenport, John Davies, John Edgington, Bruce Ellis, Kenneth Field, Ken Grainger, David Hibbert, Roger Horn, Bill Hudson, David Ibbotson, Barry Lane, Bert Lloyd, Manchester Central Library, Manchester Town Hall (City Engineer's Archives), J.R.Morten, National Railway Museum, Jim Peden, Keith Pirt, John Ryan, Mike Spick at Sheffield City Library, Jeremy Suter, Peter Ward, Roy Welch and Jeff Wells.

WOODHEAD

-- PART TWO --
DUNFORD BRIDGE, PENISTONE,
SHEFFIELD VICTORIA
and via the Worsborough Branch to Wath

Until the opening of the new Woodhead Tunnel, in June 1954, the summit of the Great Central's Manchester to Sheffield line fell just past milepost 22 - calibrated from Manchester London Road - from where the alignment had risen almost continuously. This constantly ascending grade coincided with the exit from the notorious Woodhead Tunnel. From the mouth of the tunnel through Dunford Bridge, the gradient fell at 1 in 135 to Hazelhead, then at 1 in 124/130 towards Bullhouse and Penistone. Through Huddersfield Junction at 1 in 100 to Barnsley Junction, where the lines to Barnsley and Wath ran off eastwards; the railway of the Victorian pioneers fell on a continuous down grade through the lesser tunnel at Thurgoland, Wortley, Deepcar, Oughty Bridge and Wadsley Bridge and on towards the centre of Britain's one-time premier steel-making city, Sheffield.

Rail services to Sheffield from Manchester had begun with due ceremony on December 22nd 1845. Although Sheffield's Victoria station has always been synonymous with Woodhead services, it was to a station at Bridgehouses, some ¼ mile to the north-west of Victoria, that the railway first arrived. As at the Manchester end of the line, the station at Sheffield was a simple affair; consisting originally of a mere single platform. Bridgehouses remained the terminus of the line until 1851 when the Victoria station opened. By this time the SAuL&M had become the MS&L and lines to both Gainsborough and Grimsby had opened.

A timetable for January, 1846 - the first full year that the line was in operation - shows seven through trains (Up) between Manchester and Sheffield and a corresponding number Down. This dropped to three each way on Sundays. By modern standards the journeys seem incredibly long. The first Up train left Manchester at 8.00 in the morning and did not arrive in Sheffield until 10.13., Furthermore, three trains were "all stations" affairs

Longdendale Valley showing well the scene over the Woodhead line in the immediate post-Grouping era. This time the master has selected a passenger train; drawn by ex-Great Central Atlantic No **5360**, a Manchester to Marylebone express has cleared Crowden and is passing Woodhead Reservoir-just approaching milepost 18. The six coaches are all ex-GC vehicles; the locomotive presents a fine sight in lined LNER Apple Green. No 5360 had been given a superheater boiler in October 1920-notice the earlier position of the snifting valves, alongside the chimney. In the background a freight train on the Down Goods line (loop) waits for the road at Crowden Home signal before proceeding along to Torside and Valehouse.

H.Gordon Tidey

making no less than seventeen stops! One hour and twenty-five minutes was the fastest time; this being the 10.15 Up morning train which arrived in Sheffield at 11.40.

A contrast is provided by a study of an MS&L "Time Table" of April 1877. By now the railway between Manchester and Sheffield had entered its fourth decade of operation and the country's rail map was almost complete; save, of course, for the MS&L's thrust south fuelled by Watkin's expansionist ideas. Up services began at 5.45 a.m., the first train arriving in Sheffield at 8.10. The pedestrian pace was dictated by the fact that this service was an "all stations" and a true "Stopper". Every station on the line was a port of call, making no less than 20 stops in the process. The first of what could be loosely called "express" services left London Road one hour later, at 6.45, and reached Sheffield Victoria at 7.55. Stops on this service were made at Guide Bridge, Godley Junction (connections from Stockport Tiviot Dale) and Penistone (connections for Barnsley, Doncaster and Great Grimsby). At 1 hour and 10 minutes this was the fastest train of the day, though others managed the journey in 1 hour, 11 and 12 minutes respectively.

Coming Down to Manchester, twelve weekday trains were provided. The service from Sheffield began at 6.00 a.m. Like its Up crack of dawn counterpart, this was another "all stations" service. The stop at Godley Junction, at 7.40, shows a connection for Liverpool via Stockport Tiviot Dale; this arrived in Liverpool Central at 10.10. Arrival at Manchester London Road was at 8.00. The "crack" Down train was the 9.00 a.m. departure from Sheffield Victoria. This stopped only at Penistone (at 9.21) and then ran non-stop to London Road where arrival was at 10.05. Footnotes to the timetable show some interesting features: two Down trains daily are shown as stopping at Wortley *when required to take up passengers for Manchester and Liverpool.* Passengers on the 5.48 p.m. arrival at Sheffield from Hull were reminded to.. *change carriages at Sheffield, and will be conveyed forward by the train leaving that station at 6.34 p.m.* These poor souls, having left Hull at 2.10 p.m., arrived in Manchester at 8.40. A further footnote decreed that: *passengers to Liverpool (Lime Street) will have to cross the town at Manchester between London Road and Victoria Stations at their own expense.* Lime Street was reached at 10.20; the total journey time from Hull totalling just 8 hours and 10 minutes!

Fares between Manchester and Sheffield of 120 years ago make interesting reading. Three classes of travel are shown ordinarily: 1st class, 2nd class and "Gov". The latter referred to the "Parliamentary" services - a long forgotten innovation wrought by Gladstone's Railway Regulaton Act of 1844. Under this legislation the railway companies were required to run at least one 3rd class train per day over all their lines. Parliamentary trains had to run at not less than 12 mph, must call at all stations and it was stipulated that carriages should offer protection from the weather. Fares could not exceed 1d per mile. Even 2nd class travel between the two northern cities 120 years ago was not a cheap proposition. A return ticket cost 9/2d; 1st class 12/6d; "Gov" was 6/10d. A peculiarity was the "Market Day" ticket. These were offered (on Market days only) between specific stations. One example - Penistone to Sheffield - cost 4/4d (1st class), 3/0d (2nd class) and 2/1d (4th [sic] class). In case it be thought that these fares look ridiculously cheap, their scale needs to be put into the context of contemporary wages. In 1873, four years before the currency of our time table, railwaymen's wages were in the region of 1 to 34/- per week and railwaymen, though never at the top of the national pay scale, were by no means at the bottom. Well before the First War, a Government Earnings and Hours enquiry into the building trades showed average weekly earnings of around 33/- per week in the northern counties and 38/- in London. Adult agricultural workers in 1902 earned just 17/5d per week (inclusive of all allowances in kind).

Whilst this volume looks primarily at the railway and associated branches between Manchester and Sheffield it must be remembered that in 1897 this line became also the northern part of a great trunk line. For it was on March 15th 1899 that the Great Central began regular passenger services over its London Extension and what hitherto, the Manchester, Sheffield and Lincolnshire Railway - a cross-country provincial line, was now one of the the country's railway "Greats" and ready to take on no less than three competitors for the lucrative London to Manchester passenger and goods traffic.

Manchester to London via Sheffield - before 1899

Whilst browsing through our "time table" of 120 years ago it is timely to reflect that through travel from Manchester to London over MS&L metals via Woodhead had been possible for over forty years. The MS&L in partnership with the Great Northern Railway began through services from King's Cross to Manchester on August 1st 1857 - the year of the celebrated Manchester Art Treasures Exhibition at a site near to what was then Old Trafford Station. The aim was for the Great Northern to capture some of the traffic from the hostile London & North Western and to break the latter's monopoly in the process. Such activity on the part of the upstart MS&L so angered the LNWR that passengers arriving off London trains from King's Cross via Sheffield were arrested!

For several years there were some five trains in each direction between King's Cross and Manchester. Initially the journey time was set at 5 hours 20 minutes. In 1877, the year we looked at earlier, the first Up train left Manchester London Road at 10.00a.m. Guide Bridge was reached ten minutes later, Penistone at 10.46. Departing Sheffield at 11.15, the London train called at Retford (11.35-11.50) where engines were changed at that time. Further stops were made at Newark (12.31), Grantham (12.34), Peterborough (1.15) and Huntingdon (2.45). Arrival at London King's Cross was at 3.00.

Later, the fastest train did the journey in 4¾ hours, a similar travelling time to that provided by the Midland and the LNWR. In 1883, at the behest of Sir Edward Watkin, the MS&L's dynamic Chairman, the Manchester to King's Cross trains were further accelerated when the journey time was reduced to 4½ hours; stops were now made only at Sheffield and Grantham. Just a year later, in 1884, the 2.00 p.m. trains in each direction between the two cities were further advanced-the journey time being reduced now to just 4¼ hours. These trains were at that time reputed to be the fastest in the world; the Down train reaching Grantham in just under two hours and producing an average speed of 53½ mph. On the Up journey, the 54 mph average between Grantham and King's Cross was certainly the fastest in the country at the time. Most of these services, incidentally, carried through carriages for Bradford which travelled via Penistone and Huddersfield over the L&Y system.

This joint service was certainly a most enterprising one and led to the introduction of special rolling stock; joint expenditure between the two companies resulting in the production of lavishly equipped Dining and Sleeping cars. Both the MS&L and

GNR had invested in the Victoria Hotel which adjoined the same-named station in Sheffield. The MS&L assumed sole ownership in 1883 when they bought out the GNR's share.

The abolition of the Retford stop had led to an alteration in the arrangements for locomotive working between the two companies. Prior to 1883, Retford had been the place where engines were changed, the GNR providing the motive power between here and King's Cross, the MS&L correspondingly handling things north of Retford to Manchester via Sheffield. With an engine change at Grantham, distances became a little more equitable; the GNR's 105½ miles to King's Cross equating roughly with the MS&L's 97¼ miles from Grantham to Manchester London Road. Geographically, though, the MS&L crews got the thick end of the stick;. their journey in the Up direction having to cope with the ascent to and through the Woodhead Tunnel. Neither was returning to Manchester a sinecure either; the eastern portal of Woodhead Tunnel, just beyond Dunford Bridge, was almost 1,000 feet above sea - level reached by gradients varying from 1 in 120 to 1 in 132 over the 18½ miles from Sheffield Victoria.

On March 15th 1899, coincidental with the opening of services over the GCR's London Extension, the GNR began its own services from Manchester Central to King's Cross. Not that even this was the end of the Joint services. Through coaches were coupled to the 3.40 p.m. Express from Manchester London Road, detached at Sheffield, and worked forward to Grantham by a Neepsend engine. Manchester, then the centre of the U.K's cotton trade and a city with a vast amount of manufacturing capacity, particularly in the Engineering trades, was a lucrative proposition for the railways. Indeed, the GNR went as far as building special 4'coach trains for its Manchester services in August 1906. These trains, designated "Special Through Dining Car Expresses", covered the Down journey in 4 hours with one stop at Sheffield Victoria. But, even in those palmy days, four contenders for the trunk services were, perhaps, just one too many.

In 1910 the GNR service had shrunk to two trains per day each way with a best time of 4 hours, 3 minutes Down. Other timings of 5 hours, 12 minutes and 5 hours, 30 minutes Up suggest that the company had given up the ghost as far as London to Manchester traffic was concerned. Subsequently the day ser-

Grantham Station, c.1896/97: A superb study of MS&L No. **694** as she waits on the west side of the station to take over a Down King's Cross to Manchester Express via Sheffield. The engine was built at Gorton in July, 1895 and was the first of a class of six locomotives with 7'-0" coupled wheels built up to December that year. Designated Class 11, they were based on a design by Thomas Parker of 1893. Harry Pollitt, who succeeded Thomas Parker in 1894, made minor alterations to the design. Allocated to Gorton when built, No. 694 and her five sisters are reckoned to have worked the joint London expresses for only two years before being displaced by the later Pollitt piston valved 4-4-0's-the Class 11A. The Class 11 exhibited the use for the first time on an MS&L passenger engine of a Belpaire firebox, though this had made its debut on No. 7 of Class 9C (N5) 0-6-2 tank of 1893. No. **694** is seen is "as built" condition, itself something of a rarity. A Stovepipe chimney with beaded lip, tall twin-pillar safety valves, two whistles and a tender without a coal guard-all are features dating from construction. Notice the polished steelwork-guard irons, buffer heads and coupling hook, wheel tyres and smokebox fastenings; all have received meticulous attention from the cleaners. All-in-all the locomotive gleams to perfection-witness the patterns worked up in the film of grease on the tender tank side, a true touch of pre-Group patina. What a splendid sight this locomotive must have made as she charged up the 1in-100 to 1in-132 bank from Sheffield Victoria towards Dunford Bridge and into the Woodhead tunnel. Our Manchester-bound engine appears in the later MS&L lighter green livery which was adopted around the time that Pollitt succeeded Parker. The main body colour was edged in chocolate brown, lined yellow. The brown was extended to the front raised framing, the running plate angles, footsteps, buffer casings and tender frames. Locomotive splashers were edged in polished brass. Notice the lamps, features most elegantly styled. Such large specimens do not seem to have survived into the Great Central era. The engine headcode is for an Express Passenger working-noted from the 1896 WTT appendices and thus helping to date the photograph. *Author's collection*

Grantham, c.1892-95: Forming a contrast to our study of the superb No. 694 is MS&LR Class 2 4-4-0 No. **685** standing at the north end of Grantham station at the head of a King's Cross to Manchester express via Sheffield. Judging by the shadows on the photograph the train may well be the 10.10 a.m. departure from King's Cross which was due here at 12.32 (and where engines were changed). With a stop at Retford (1.15), the 10.10 was due in Sheffield Victoria at 1.53 and was away again three minutes later. Further stops at Penistone (2.20), Godley Junction (2.50) and Guide Bridge (2.58) brought arrival in Manchester London Road at 3.10. In the previous decade, on February 4th 1886, a Gorton passenger engine diagram showed Driver G. Tindale and Fireman P. Burgess booking on at 8.30 a.m. with Sacré Single No. 507 to work the 10.00 departure from Manchester London Road as far as Grantham. The men returned with the 12.00 noon from King's Cross due at Grantham at 3.14. Tindale and Burgess were due back in London Road at 6.00 and booked off duty at 6.15 p.m. This diagram allowed the men 2lb. of tallow, 6 ¼ quarts of oil and ½ lb. of cotton waste for their engine. The economics of travel in the following decade (1877) lists an Ordinary Return ticket from Manchester to London over this route as costing, 1st Class 49/-; 2nd Class 40/- and 3rd Class 30/11d. *Author's collection*

vices were replaced by one overnight express in each direction. These reached Manchester via Godley Junction, Woodley, Stockport Tiviot Dale and then over the Manchester South District line into Central Station.

At the beginning of 1917 these overnight trains ceased to carry passengers, becoming instead Parcel trains. By 1920, though, even these services had disappeared. The GNR's presence over the Woodhead line via Sheffield had ended - at least as far as passengers were concerned. Not that this had finished GN involvement in Manchester, far from it. The company had opened its massive Deansgate Goods Warehouse in July 1898 a development which must have given the rival companies - the LNWR, GCR and Midland something of a shudder.

But despite their ultimate demise, the Manchester-King's Cross expresses had laid the foundation stone for top-link MS&L motive power. The company, fired by Edward Watkin's ruthlessness and determination, was to acquire its own route to London.

The Manchester to Marylebone trains that passed over Woodhead from 1899 onwards would be hauled by a succession of motive power as varied and as impressive as anything on any north to south trunk route. First Pollitt and then Robinson 4-4-0's, Atlantics, "Sir Sams", "Directors", the 9P 4-6-0's, with "Valour" as its most honoured member, the Gresley "Sandringhams" and the redoubtable A1 and A3 Pacifics. Finally to the Thompson B1 and then to the modern Electric locomotive - at least as far as Sheffield.

Manchester to Sheffield via Woodhead had a difficult birth and, sadly, not a long life. But what it lacked in longevity, it made up for in variety, fascination, panache, even brilliance. I hope you will agree.

E. M. Johnson,
Burnage, Manchester.
January 1998.

The Western Side Revisited

As mentioned in the Foreword, much new material came to light dealing with Woodhead - some of it almost before the books were on the shelves! So, to refresh reader's palates, so to speak, here is a little resume showing a few treats on the western side of the line up to, once again, the mouth of that historic tunnel.

(Left) Woodhead, early 1950s: In the immediate run up to electrification in 1954, the Thompson B1 seems to have been the mainstay of express working between Manchester and Sheffield. Giving us a last glimpse of the western portal of the tunnel, No. **61156** emerges into the daylight and begins the 19 or so miles drift downhill towards Manchester. Behind the train, work appears to be well in hand on the new tunnel. Interestingly, No. 61156 appears to have left Gorton Works without the "Lion and Wheel" crest on the tender tank side. *P. Ward*

Woodhead Signalbox, c.1947: This picture was used in volume I and was made from a rather poor copy. Amazingly, the original negative turned up after going to press, thus enabling much more detail to be obtained. Perusal of line plans prior to the turn of the century show a somewhat different layout at Woodhead to that of modern times. The mid 1890's to 1908 saw extensive provision of Loops (or Goods Lines) installed on the western side of the tunnel mouth between Valehouse and Woodhead. Up Loops were installed at Woodhead itself in 1895 and 1900; though whether the latter year saw a lengthening of the existing provision is uncertain. The MS&L line plan of 1884, drawn by Henry Fowler, Surveyor of King Street, Manchester, shows two signalboxes here at Woodhead. One, Woodhead West, was sited on the Up side of the line 10 chains east of milepost 18½. This box controlled the exit from a Down loop and a trailing crossover. Terminating just short of this box, on the Up side of the line, was set of 10 sidings designated "Woodhead Relief Sidings." A second box, Woodhead East - also on the Down side was situated 2½ chains west of the end of the station platform. Thus, with a degree of certainty, this signalbox, with its brick base, can be dated from sometime between 1895 and 1900. The massive water tank, visible behind the Up platform and a feature seen here for many years, is shown on the early plan and is listed as holding 66,000 gallons. An interesting peculiarity at Woodhead was that each side of the station was in a different county. The north (Up) platform and water tank were located in Cheshire, the south (Down) platform and all the adjacent buildings were actually in Derbyshire! Notice the sand drags within the formation of the Up line into which runaway vehicles from the rising 1-in-201 gradient through the tunnel could be directed should the need arise.

Author's collection

Hyde Junction, n.d: We viewed the scene here *(Part One; page 75)* at the onset of electrification and an earlier view *(Part One; page 76)* showed operations at ground - level. This time, from Hyde Junction box, we are able to take a "signalman's eye view" of Class D11 No. **5511** *Marne* approaching the junction with an Up express. The tracks seen above the retaining wall to the right were part of Hyde Junction sidings and left the Up line alongside Daniel Admanson & Co's works. A further line from these sidings ran round to take traffic to and from the adjacent Victoria Colliery. The MS&L line plan of 1884 shows the small buildings in front of the mill as being a Signal and Telegraph works belonging to Messrs.Stevens & Sons.
GCRS collection

East of Godley Junction, 1938: Godley Junction was an important focal point in the Woodhead theatre of operations. Here traffic to and from Merseyside was interchanged from the CLC to the GCR and vice-versa. Those of us fortunate to have seen steam operations over the CLC in the 1950's know just how much traffic must have been handled here at Godley. In 1938 Manchester Locomotive Society member Gerald Harrop visited Godley to take these splendid views - here and on the page opposite. Perhaps rather unusually, Gerry went off station limits to do so. Though exact dates are not known for these photographs, the trio of views provides an excellent example of the variety of motive power to be seen over Woodhead in the years before the Second War.

(Below) Godley Junction station is seen clearly in the background as D11 Director No. **5503** *Somme*, in the rather sombre black livery of the period, runs past at the head of an 8 - coach Up express. At this time *Somme* belonged to Gorton, but by then Directors had been displaced, to the reputed chagrin of Gorton drivers, by B17s.

(Above) A vantage point a little further up the line shows off one of Şomme's successors - a B17 No. **2856** *Leeds United* resplendent in lined apple green hauling another 8 - coach express, this time almost certainly bound for Marylebone. No. 2856 was completed at Darlington in 1936 and spent a brief period at Neasden. In 1938 she was allocated to Leicester before finishing up at Cambridge in May 1939. Thereafter she remained in East Anglia and was cut up in 1960.

(Below) Though this picture is a trifle flawed technically, I find it the most attractive of the three. K3 No. **1300** roars past the camera, and some rather interesting Private Owner wagons, and heads towards Godley East and Hattersley cutting. Passengers gazing from the Gresley brake third behind the tender draw our attention to the train; the remainder of the stock is certainly worth a mention. Two corridor thirds and a further brake third complete the first part of the ensemble. Behind this can be seen a six wheeled vehicle with a guard's ducket to the rear-possibly an ex-MS&L vehicle. Vehicle No. 6 is of a non-passenger type, probably a luggage van. Another Gresley vehicle is glimpsed to the rear of this whilst bringing up the rear is a Great Western coach. An altogether remarkable ensemble! The stopping passenger headcode poses food for thought. No. 1300 had two allocations in 1938, being based at both York and Retford. *G. Harrop/Author's collection*

(Left) Hattersley Cutting, 1930's: In volume one we saw the enormous civil engineering enterprise involved in opening out the two tunnels at Hattersley to form the vast cutting, part of which can be glimpsed again here. B7 No. 5471 charges through the cutting at speed with an Up stopping train-notice the solitary headlamp and the non-corridor stock.

Joe Lloyd/GCRS collection

Broadbottom Viaduct, n.d: A winter scene at this historic spot as the Manchester to Glossop push-pull set crosses the River Etherow and heads towards Dinting. The shallow stone-arched bridge at the base of the viaduct carries the Broadbottom to Charlesworth road over the river. January 1st 1857: Report by Engineer R. Russell: "The tie-rods which you authorised me last summer to put into the Etherow Viaduct have fully answered my expectation. They have given me entire command over the arches and enabled me to straighten the lines of rails over the viaduct, and have added very much to the stiffness of the structure. The lateral vibration is now scarcely perceptible. The work has been carefully and well done by Mr. Taylor. The timber, whenever cut into, has proved to be perfectly sound. The scaffolding has not yet been removed, and I shall let it remain for some days, in case any of the Directors wish to examine the work." Extract from MSL Board minute.

Peter Ward

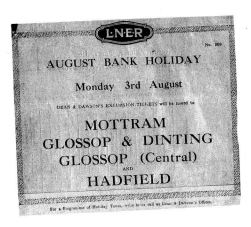

(Below) Glossop Station 1951: C13 No. 67417 rests in Glossop station prior to returning to Manchester with the two coach push-pull set. Raising of the platforms appears to have taken place as a possible prelude to electrification. No. 67417 was taken out of service in January 1960-the last of the C13's to be withdrawn having seen a working life of almost 57 years. **C. H. A. Townley/J. Peden**

Dinting Station, n.d: A view of the main line platform looking towards the viaduct with Hadfield behind the photographer. The footbridge was obviously covered in at this time; unfortunately, it has not been possible to ascertain when the coverings were removed. Dinting station signalbox, seen here, looks a relatively new structure in this photograph. A clue lies with the map from the 1884 line survey. This shows the station signalbox at that time as being sited at the west end of this platform and behind the footbridge, i.e. in the fork of what was then the new formation-the triangular junction with the Glossop Branch. Perhaps unusually, the old box stood at something of a right-angle to the main line and faced out towards Dinting viaduct. **Courtesy of John Davies**

Snowbound Over Woodhead

The wild and exposed nature of the Pennine moorland made the Woodhead line particularly susceptible to bad weather conditions. Writers dealing with the railway have variously implicated almost every station east of Hadfield as being the most exposed or the bleakest place to wait for a train in winter. Both railwaymen and seasoned travellers over the line will hold their own views on what was the prize location for bad weather or difficult operating conditions. My own contender would be Mottram Yard; having visited the place in the depths of winter, the very thought of men working out in such exposed conditions makes one shiver!

But, maybe, travellers and enthusiasts are not the hardiest or most experienced of souls when it comes to dealing with atrocious weather conditions. With this in mind, I asked Benny McVey, a former railwayman with almost half a century's experience of working on the Woodhead line, to recount for us the conditions he experienced at Dunford Bridge in the atrocious winter of 1947.

"As far as I can remember the awful winter of 1947, I think the ferocity of the blizzard began in the January, I recall about the 25th. The very strong winds drifted the snow all along the hillside from Dunford to the top of the hill. I used to have a photo of me and a few more men stood on the top of the telegraph poles which were just to be seen above the snow. We had to make our way from Dunford to Townhead across the moors; it (the snow) was about 20-30 feet thick on the main road. The overhead electric wires were down so we had no electricity in our house for 9 weeks. When one lived here at Dunford you always had to prepare for a bad winter. We cooked on a Primus stove; we had no wireless and the roads were closed while an American bulldozer cleared them. My wife was stuck in the house for 9 weeks and was unable to get

out. Fortunately, we had plenty of coal as we used to have it delivered by the ton along by the Stanhope Arms; the owner's son was in the coal business. I remember sheep being brought out of the drifts after 6 or 7 weeks-it was awful. The railway was at a standstill for a week or so and trains were buried, especially between Woodhead and Torside. The other bad winter was around the middle of February 1940. I tramped from Dunford to Holmfirth with a friend of mine in a ferocious snowstorm-up to the knees we were. We were going to register for military service; we were 24 years old. We left Dunford at 8.00 in the morning to arrive in Holmfirth at 1.00. We got back home at 11.00 that night! The man at the Labour Exchange where we had to register told us we were crackers to have come. But what could you do, when it told you in the letter that failure to register meant going to jail. Sadly, my friend was called up and was killed in action in 1942".

Hadfield, n.d: The first coal train passes through the station after the worst of the drifts had been cleared. *Railway Gazette*

To return to 1947: The Glossop Chronicle carried a lengthy report detailing how the town and the surrounding areas had been hit by the worst winter since 1933. The newspaper reported hurricane-like snowstorms on Sunday and Monday, January 26th and 27th, which ties in more or less exactly with Benny's account. The newspaper recounts the railway's plight thus: "Pushing its way through a mass of built-up drifts, a train plough chugged its way into Hadfield station on Wednesday afternoon to mark the end of a thirty-hour struggle to clear the Manchester-Sheffield line. Throughout Tuesday night, local railwaymen and Polish soldiers worked feverishly. As soon as the snow was shovelled away new drifts formed, but at 1.00am. on Wednesday morning, after six hours, the Polish troops returned to their Lancashire stations, their job done. As a result of their work and that of local men, the line between Hadfield and Dinting was cleared and almost normal services were running to Manchester on Wednesday.

Earlier, railwaymen had dug out an engine carrying (sic) two empty coaches which became wedged in the drift. At 2.00 a.m. on Tuesday, special linesmen were rushed by special train from Manchester to dig out snowdrifts. On the blocked by-line between Dinting and Glossop, gangs of menworked to clear the line, and on Wednesday afternoon an engine was able to reach Glossop. Last train to reach Glossop before that was at 10.15 p.m. on Monday night, and since then, Manchester passengers from Glossop have travelled by a special bus to Dinting.

On Tuesday night, several trains were snowbound beyond Hadfield. At Valehouse, a parcels train lay submerged in an outsize drift. Earlier, four railwaymen had collapsed from exposure. Hours were spent in re-railing wagons and coaches which had become de-railed in clearing the snow. A restaurant car brought up to serve hot drinks and food to the men was among those which had become de-railed. And while men were righting it, the train that they had dug out became buried again.

Two and a half weeks later, on Friday, February 14th, the newspaper carried a report stating that: "..... train services between Manchester and Sheffield should be approaching something like normal for the first time in two weeks as at 1.30am., On Wednesday, both tracks were reported to be clear. Over 750 men were employed between Tuesday last week and Wednesday morning this week to dig away the swirling drifts of snow that settled across the line between Dinting and Woodhead. The work of 300 Poles who cleared the line on Tuesday night last week was undone by Saturday and 200 German prisoners of war were brought in to move the freshly-formed drifts. Another heavy fall of snow on Sunday played havoc with the work already done and disorganised attempts to send coal supplies through to Manchester from the other side of the Woodhead Tunnel. Two hundred Pioneer Corps men worked through Monday and Tuesday and were assisted by fifty unemployed workers from Glossop. The work of clearing the line had achieved top priority and an order direct from the Government said the line had to be cleared at all costs. Several train loads that became derailed in the operations hindered the clearance work. Yesterday (Thursday) several trains were travelling on both lines to and from Sheffield and a few coal trains and empty wagon loads (sic) will be able to pass along the line".

Dunford Bridge, n.d: The scene looking east towards the sorting sidings. German prisoners of war (presumably those who had not been repatriated) helped in snow-clearing operations. *Railway Gazette*

Valehouse, c.1899: Retrieved from a very rare and somewhat scarred original, this view shows Pollitt Class 11A 4-4-0 No. **269** heading an Up express past Valehouse signalbox and towards Torside. The train is reputedly one of the first through GCR passenger workings from Manchester to Marylebone. The coaches have French Grey upper panels, abandoned in favour of cream towards the end of 1903. Close by the locomotive, the signal on the Up line carries a bracket arm, note the ring denoting a goods line, for the loop or goods line operational between Valehouse and Torside from October 17th 1898. The bridge in the background is numbered 61 (*cf volume I*), Hadfield East box can just be discerned in front, close by the tall bracket signal.
Courtesy of John Davies

Wilf Ward, Permanent Way Inspector, Guide Bridge to Penistone, c.1938: Inevitably, much of the focus on railwaymen has tended to centre around footplate crews. Though the locomotive was the prime mover on the railway, its running and existence depended upon the work of many, many other men, people who, I feel, have seldom been referred to in print. Wilf Ward, seen here on the Woodhead side of the tunnel, was accustomed to walking two of his lengths every day and on Saturday mornings would travel to Penistone on the footplate of an express. Carrying with him 20 or so wooden pegs, each about a foot long, when he encountered a bad spot of track he would drop one of these pegs off the engine. Thus was devised a simple system of informing the ganger as to where rough spots of track were to be found. The total number of pegs would be reported back so that, on Sundays, the necessary remedial maintenance could be carried out. Wilf Ward lived in the crossing house on Dinting Lane. His wife, Annie, was the crossing keeper from 1931 to 1952 and here the couple raised 13 children. Benny McVey, a lifelong railwayman who spent many years working on the Woodhead line, would like this photograph to serve as a tribute to Wilf Ward who he describes thus: "He was the one who put me on my feet at 21 after suffering years of unemployment". Wilf Ward died on March 12th.1964.
Collection of Benny McVey

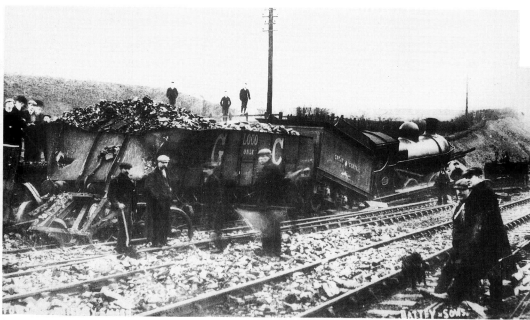

Torside, n.d: Taken from a contemporary postcard published by Battey & Sons and entitled "Torside Railway Smash" this picture shows "Pom-Pom" No. **1118** in deep trouble at the end of the headshunt from the Down goods line. One suspects the train became out of control on the falling 1-in-117 gradient. The 40-ton steel-bodied bogie loco coal wagon at the front of the train has withstood the impact well, but one wooden-bodied coal wagon has been catapulted over the locomotive and lies, bottom up, several feet in front. Coal is scattered everywhere and, no doubt, a considerable amount of gleaning took place afterwards!
GCRS Collection

(Opposite) Torside, May 12th 1945: Definitely a photograph that should not have been taken! War Office restrictions prohibited railway photography from September 1939 onwards. The Second War was still raging when our intrepid photographer caught O4 No. **5331** at the head of a train of tanks moving along the Down line just past Torside Crossing and approaching milepost 15. Notice the overhead stanchions for the catenary; erected in 1938, electrification was a long way off indeed at this time.   *G. Harrop/Author's collection*

Crowden, June 16th 1936: As mentioned in the companion volume, Manchester Corporation had been heavily engaged in reservoir building in the Longdendale Valley in the mid-years of the nineteenth century. Adjacent to Crowden station, a latecomer to the Woodhead line, having opened in 1861, were two reservoirs-Torside and Woodhead-separated by an embankment over which runs the B6105 road from Glossop. In this fine panorama, the photographer stands overlooking the sluice which channelled water down from Torside to the Woodhead reservoir in the distance. Taking centre stage is Crowden station with the four railway cottages-dwellings built by the MS&L for their employees-overlooking the platforms. Leading from the cottages to the station is a footpath bordered by a post and rail fence which drops down to the fine lattice footbridge spanning the four tracks. Glancing along, beginning in the small goods yard, the diminutive crane, used when wagonloads arrived "by arrangement only", stands out. Crowden's fine brick buildings, reminiscent of a Nonconformist chapel, were a symbol of an age of optimism when rail travel was king. Notice, too, the fine array of Great Central semaphores-no less than six can be seen-and of course the splendid GCR signalbox with its back to us and facing the running lines. Nearer the camera, the men from the Waterworks have assembled their tools: even a set of miniature rails and sleepers has been made ready. Obviously, this is going to be quite a big job. Clearing the station and blasting its way up towards Woodhead is a mixed freight train, the Up Loop signal pegged off to allow its noisy progress and only the rasping roar of a steam engine hard at work disturbs the tranquility. However, the sheep in the foreground seem unperturbed, the tinkle of the thirsty watercourse runs on down and the train will soon disappear into the haze beyond.   *Manchester City Engineers Archive*

Off the rails at Woodhead

Woodhead, July 23rd 1951
(Upper) The Gorton breakdown crane, a Ransomes type, has been summoned to the assistance of B1 No. **61162**. On entering the crossover after working "wrong line" through the tunnel, the engine's bogie has become derailed. Lifting shackles are in place and the crane gets ready to lift the stricken engine so the bogie can be manoeuvred back onto the rails.

(Lower) All has now been righted and the chains are raised clear of the locomotive. No less than 22 men can be seen in this picture, all no doubt had a part to play. One can only marvel at the speed and efficiency of the breakdown gangs of yesterday. Today, even the slightest whiff of trouble seems to ensure the prompt dispatch of passengers into hired buses and taxis followed by closures that seem to last for days.   *B. W. L. Brooksbank*

Three Views at Woodhead, 1930's: (Left-Upper) Ex-Robinson ROD 2-8-0 No. **6602** pulls out of the Up loop with a lengthy train of coal empties being returned to the Yorkshire pits. As mentioned before, a remarkably unfamiliar sight that must have been seen countless times before, but photographed how often? Much has been written about the "glories" of steam, but one wonders how many writers would care to have taken a daily trip through the suffocating conditions endured by footplate crews through the Woodhead Tunnel. **(Centre)** A sparkling B17, No. **2862** *Manchester United,* passes the box at the head of the 3.52 p.m. stopping passenger train from Manchester London Road to Sheffield Victoria. Known to signalmen as the "Sheffield Ord" the train called at Gorton, Guide Bridge, Newton, Godley Junction (where two minutes were allowed), Mottram, Dinting, Hadfield and then all stations to Sheffield where arrival was booked for 5.37. **(Lower)** To complete the trio a second GC engine makes its appearance in the form of No. **5194**, the second of the first two Robinson Atlantics completed by Beyer, Peacock & Co. in December 1903. The engine, somewhat grimy in appearance, charges through the station in fine style at the head of an eight coach Up express. *all R. K. Blencowe collection*

Dunford Bridge

Dunford Bridge, c.1932: A view taken from the Windleden Lane overbridge (No. 71) and looking west towards the portals of the Woodhead Tunnel. The driver of a Class B7/2 4-6-0 glances backwards as his engine moves ahead towards the beckoning gloom of the Down tunnel. To the right of the picture, the Dunford No. 1 Up Home signal, with its typical GC features, must have gladdened the hearts of many a driver over the years as their engines emerged into fresh air and daylight once again - the three mile uphill choking slog now over. Notice the facing connection being installed to allow "wrong line" working through the tunnel when maintenance was being carried out. It is not known when this connection was installed. The 1884 line survey shows no crossover here; a 6 - chain shunting neck projected back from the Up line towards the tunnel mouth at this time.

D. Ibbotson

Dunford Bridge, looking west, June 5th. 1954: Possibly one of the last photographs taken of a train emerging out of the old Woodhead Tunnel. On Sunday, June 13th all traffic through the tunnels was suspended whilst the work of connecting the trackwork through the new tunnel to the existing system on either side was undertaken. Typifying freight operations along the line an unidentified Class 04/8 moves its train of empty coal wagons out of the Up tunnel complete with a trail of smoke and exhaust in its wake. Notice the Home signal has been moved to a lower level in the intervening years and now stands on the "wrong" side of the line to improve sighting. The facing crossover also enabled banking engines to cross back over to the Up line after giving a "shove" up the bank from Barnsley Junction, Penistone. At least one amusing incident of bankers forgetting to "hook off" is recorded resulting in an enforced trip through the tunnel !

Ken Boulter

Dunford from the air (n.d)

Reproduced from a picture postcard, this view looks south with the railway running across on a west to east axis from right to left giving a bird's eye aspect of Dunford Bridge. Cutting in from the top right - hand corner is the old Turnpike road that leads from today's A628 Manchester to Sheffield road through the Woodhead pass. The former Turnpike connects with the B6106 Holmfirth to Penistone road at Carlecotes. Known here as Windleden Lane, this thoroughfare crossed the railway at right - angles. Standing prominently above the railway (look for the three chimney stacks) are the six cottages on Windleden Lane that once housed various railway employees - see the Tidey view showing the J11. Plainly visible on the Up platform are the large water tank, station buildings and Dunford No. 1 signalbox (at the bottom left - hand corner). Above the Down line and hard up against the lane, is the Stationmaster's house, one - time home of Messrs. Hibbott and Grummit. Over to the left, behind the approach road to the station, is the Stanhope Arms. Dunford's "Local"; the Stanhope Arms takes its name from John Spencer Stanhope a local landowner. As part of the construction of the new Woodhead tunnel, land in front of the Stanhope Arms had to be purchased, in July 1950, from the Barnsley Brewery Company. Subsequent development in connection with the new works and station saw demolition of the stationmaster's house. It is still possible to have a drink in the Stanhope Arms today but, with the railway long gone, the surroundings seen below have changed out of all recognition.

Authors Collection

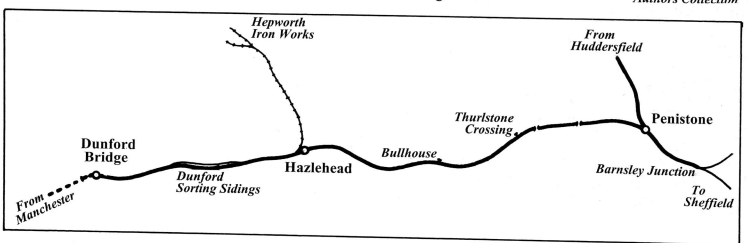

Dunford Bridge, c.1947: The stone arch of the Sheffield Road overbridge acts as a silhouette to this view of a Down express awaiting departure for Manchester with a B1 impatiently blowing off at its head. Full marks to Peter Ward for this imaginative shot showing, for a change, some interesting Gresley carriage detail as opposed to the more usual aspects of the locomotive scene. *Peter Ward*

Dunford *"Station and Staff"*

Dunford Bridge, 1920's: J11/1 "Pom Pom" No. **5232** has emerged from the eastern portal of the tunnel and passes alongside the Up platform with a through freight train, the bulk of which appears to comprise empty coal wagons. Today, when sights such as this are only seen as "special events" on some preserved railways, the appearance of a nice, clean, handsome - looking steam locomotive at the head of a long freight train would appear as something to be wondered at. Paradoxically, perhaps, what makes this picture special therefore, is that it depicts something which, at the time, was totally unremarkable; a scene that, sixty or seventy years ago, could be witnessed perhaps thirty times in one eight hour period - on almost any working day in the year. Within sight and sound of the railway were the six cottages on Windleden Lane - seen just by the bridge. The lane, known in earlier years as the "Dunford Old Turnpike Road", led from Mottram to the junction of the roads to Penistone and Barnsley and Holmfirth and Huddersfield. Owned by the railway, the cottages once housed a wagon examiner, two shunters, Harry Clay being one of the Dunford signalmen and a permanent way ganger. The dwellings were demolished around the time of the building of the new Woodhead Tunnel. *H. Gordon Tidey*

(Right)) **Dunford Bridge, March 26th.1950** The ensemble of water tank, waiting shelter and Dunford No. 1 signalbox seen from the Down platform. Dunford No. 1 box would have almost certainly dated from the opening of the sorting sidings in 1901. An earlier, smaller, signalbox stood further along the platform nearer to the road overbridge. Visible in the background is the terrace of houses standing on Windleden Lane just by the overbridge. Waiting here for a train in the winter months must have been a far from pleasant experience. At least the signalmen had the benefit of a coal - burning stove to keep them warm!
R. E. Gee

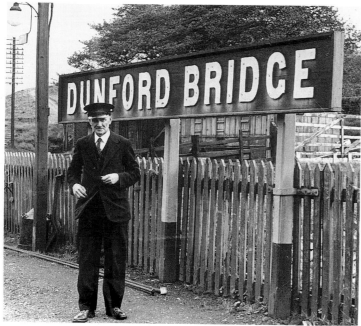

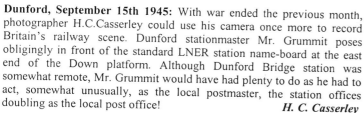

Dunford, September 15th 1945: With war ended the previous month, photographer H.C.Casserley could use his camera once more to record Britain's railway scene. Dunford stationmaster Mr. Grummit poses obligingly in front of the standard LNER station name-board at the east end of the Down platform. Although Dunford Bridge station was somewhat remote, Mr. Grummit would have had plenty to do as he had to act, somewhat unusually, as the local postmaster, the station offices doubling as the local post office!
H. C. Casserley

(Above) Dunford Bridge Station, 1925: A copy made from a battered and bruised original has yielded this little snippet of history. Posed outside Dunford No. 1 signalbox are (l to r): John E. Davies-Porter, Norman Goldthorpe-Junior porter, Miss Beatrice Ullyot-booking clerk, and Mr. T.Hibbott, at that time Station Master and Postmaster (see text). Mr.Hibbott looks every inch the part with gold braided cap, winged collar, waistcoat and the obligatory gold chain. Surveying the scene from the box window is signalman Alf Woolley.
John E. Davies

Dunford Bridge, March 18th 1950: The photographer has ignored the impending sight of a Down freight train and has provided an unusual shot showing the Down platform buildings of the old station. With the construction of the new Woodhead tunnel now under way and work soon to begin on Dunford's new station, these buildings will shortly be demolished, allowing work to begin on this, the south-east side of the line to accommodate the new station and realigned trackwork.
J. D. Darby

Dunford Bridge, 1930's: The term "Merry-go-Round" has long been applied to the modern day movement of coal from pit to power station. In pure terms, though, MGR - type operations had been working over Woodhead long before the advent of the modern coal train. What observers saw, in the main, was an endless procession of coal trains bringing coal in bulk over the Pennines from the Yorkshire pits to fuel the industry and power stations of Lancashire and Cheshire. Once the wooden bodied wagons had parted with their load, back they went to Yorkshire and the cycle began all over again. In very typical fashion, a Robinson 04 demonstrates the "Merry-go-Round" of coal operation over Woodhead in the 1930's. Coming up through Dunford Bridge, No. **6293** (one of the last of the North British - built ROD engines of 1919) has emerged from the tunnel and passes Dunford No. 1 box with an Up train of wagon empties.   *R. K. Blencowe collection*

(Left) Dunford Bridge station, pre-WWII: A most interesting picture of three characters who helped to keep this hive of activity going in the hectic days of long ago. Standing outside Dunford No 1 signalbox are (l to r): H. Clay, one of the Dunford No 1 signal men, Mr. Wild, who was Relief Stationmaster here and J. Lawton, who was one of Dunford's porters. The slot cut in the horizontal planking of the signal box was to enable the signalmen to keep a discreet eye on passengers on the platform! *Courtesy Benny McVey*

(Right) Dunford No 1 Signal box, c.1950. Signalman Wilf Carter, then a rest day relief signalman here, poses obligingly for Kenneth Field's camera at the west end of the box (the frame here was at the back). Above Alf's head can be seen the hooped satchels containing the keys for single line working through the old Woodhead Tunnels. These were passed to the fireman in time-honoured fashion, the keys working in conjunction with the SLW machine to free the appropriate block instruments. The satchels replaced a previous staff system around 1948. Single line working was usually in force for about 12 hours at a time. Notice the heavily worn wooden plank in front of the lever frame and adjacent holes in the "lino". A signalman's lot here must have been a very busy one.

Kenneth Field

Dunford Bridge, 1930's; The photographer of the view opposite was a few yards further west along the platform when another coal train, approached, climbing the last section of the 1 in 135 towards the mouth of Woodhead Tunnel. Once through the station platforms and into the tunnel, the gradient then falls all the way to Manchester.   *R. K. Blencowe collection*

On the Down side at Dunford

Dunford Bridge, October 11th 1935:
Off the road at Dunford. B8 (GCR 1A) 4-6-0, No. **5004** *Glenalmond* suffered this mishap when the driver, believed to be named Pickering from Colwick, was waiting in the Down loop from Dunford No 2 with the 11.30 p.m. Colwick to Deansgate (Manchester) Goods. Unfortunately, Driver Pickering mistook the main line signals for those of the loop and was foul of the main line when he was struck forcibly by B7 No 5476 hauling the 2.55 am Sheffield to Manchester Mail. The dire results are shown here. On this, the day after the accident, timber props are in place to shore up the stricken engine while the breakdown crane is manoeuvred into position. A plentiful supply of onlookers is in evidence as usual!
Collection of Benny McVey

Dunford Bridge Station, looking East, n.d; Making an interesting comparison with later views of the station, the entire complement of staff has turned out, or so it seems, to have their picture taken! Worthy of mention is the bracket Home signal with the ring denoting the arm controlling entry to the Up Goods loop. Notice the waiting shelter on the Up platform and the absence of Dunford No. 1 signalbox (Q. V.) The roof supports on the platform shelter are typical MS&L features and can be seen at other locations - notably Gorton, Deepcar and Hadfield.

Collection of John Davies

Dunford Bridge, June 2nd.1951: A splendid summer scene showing Dunford in transition; notice the Down platform buildings have recently been demolished prior to the building of the new station. In the background various structures have been erected to house tools and equipment for the new tunnel. On the platform below a group of six men appear to be in animated conversation - oblivious of the passing of an 04 at the head of a Down freight train. Beyond the signalbox, on the Up side of the line, the station yard appears to be handling ample traffic - clearly a fascinating place to be in those far - off years of almost half a century ago. *Collection of Roger Carpenter*

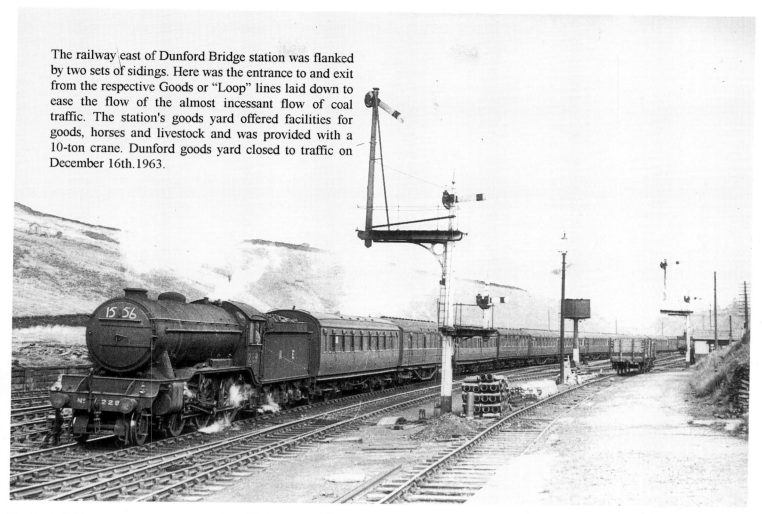

The railway east of Dunford Bridge station was flanked by two sets of sidings. Here was the entrance to and exit from the respective Goods or "Loop" lines laid down to ease the flow of the almost incessant flow of coal traffic. The station's goods yard offered facilities for goods, horses and livestock and was provided with a 10-ton crane. Dunford goods yard closed to traffic on December 16th.1963.

Dunford Bridge, September 15th. 1945: After the cessation of hostilities, the celebrated railway photographer, H. C. Casserley, lost no time getting busy with his camera to record the contemporary railway scene. This was a Saturday and K3 No. **229** with wartime "NE" on its tender and a load of at least 11 bogies is seen heading west towards the station with a Down excursion working. *H. C. Casserley*

East of Dunford Bridge, 1930's: A splendid sight is provided by the appearance of B17 No. **2840** *Somerleyton Hall* as it sweeps past the yard on a fine summer day with a Down Express. An 04 waits for the road in the loop. A fascinating touch is provided by the sight of the straw-hatted man wearing a jacket and flannels standing by the Goods line. Attired thus, he is certainly not a railwayman and both he and his companion photographer are clearly out of bounds. Was this perhaps the occasion of an SLS visit to the area?

Collection R. S. Carpenter

Dunford Bridge, early 1920s: One of two panoramic views by master photographer H. Gordon Tidey showing freight operations at Dunford. The view looks west towards the station and the tunnel mouth; the small stone depot on the south side of the River Dun and served by the goods yard here is across on the left, behind the main line. Heading east on the Up Main line, a lengthy goods train saunters along hauled by the almost obligatory Robinson 2-8-0.

H. Gordon Tidey

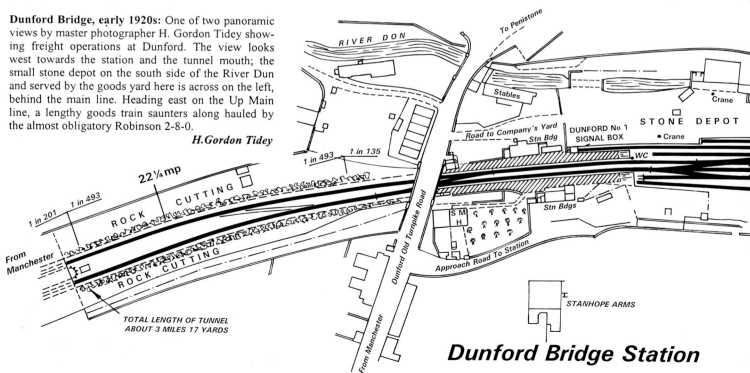

To Penistone

RIVER DON

Stables

Road to Company's Yard

DUNFORD No 1 SIGNAL BOX

Stn Bdg

STONE DEPOT

Crane

Crane

WC

22¼ mp

1 in 493   1 in 135

ROCK CUTTING

1 in 201   1 in 493

From Manchester

ROCK CUTTING

Dunford Old Turnpike Road

SM H

Stn Bdgs

Approach Road To Station

From Manchester

TOTAL LENGTH OF TUNNEL ABOUT 3 MILES 17 YARDS

STANHOPE ARMS

Dunford Bridge Station

Dunford Bridge, looking east, early 1920s: The second of the panoramas. Tidey is reputed to have holidayed at Dunford; he could have chosen many other locations, but we have cause to be grateful that he didn't. Clearly this is summer; trees are in leaf and vegetation abounds. With camera turned about, in the distance, Dunford No 2 box can be clearly seen; this controlled the entry to the reception sidings, notice the "peg" is off for the Up coal train receding out of the view. Beyond the reception sidings Dunford No 3 looked after the movement of traffic into the sorting sidings. Permissive Block working was in force along the Down Goods line; notice how the locomotive of the train in the rear has buffered right up to the Guard's van of the train in front. Once more, coal, coal and still more coal is in transit. The sidings in the foreground appear to be raised, but this is somewhat illusory; for obvious reasons the four tracks are on level ground and the main line is on a falling gradient of 1 in 135 towards Hazlehead.   *H. Gordon Tidey*

Dunford Bridge, late 1920's: An opposite hand view to the two Tidey panoramas which show, so magificently, the scene here when traffic-both passenger and freight-still abounded. "Improved Director" (GCR 11F, LNER D11) No. **5510** *Princess Mary* runs smartly past the station yard and packed Down loop with a Down Express. Clearly, this is a summer scene; bushes and trees are in full leaf, carriage windows are down and the driver sits back nonchalantly at his open cab window with half an eye on the photographer. Standing on the raised sidings over alongside the Goods lines is a former GC 15-ton 4-wheel brake van, whilst some loaded ELSECAR coal wagons in the loop add some home-brewed flavour to the picture. *Princess Mary's* express is made up of seven coaches and two vans in the rear. The coaching stock comprises GCR, ECJS and LNER vehicles. Behind the tender is a magnificent specimen; a 12-wheeled East Coast Joint Stock 61 ft. four-compartment corridor brake third. Numbered 52024, it was built at Cowlairs in 1901 to Type BC66V. Its ECJS number was 288; transferred to the former GC section in May 1927, the coach was withdrawn from service in March 1951. Notice the lengths of rail dropped in and alongside the Up siding roads-almost certainly part of the replacement stock for the track inside the Woodhead Tunnel (Q.V.)   *H. Gordon Tidey*

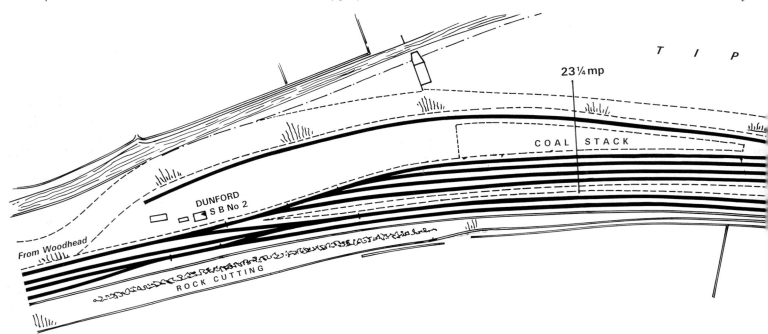

East of Dunford Bridge, late 1920's: In contrast to the earlier Robinson engines, here is an example of his last express passenger 4-6-0 and arguably the most impressive, the GCR 9P 4-6-0, LNER B3. Once the pride of Gorton, No. **6165** *Valour* heads along with a 5-coach Up express in the direction of Hazlehead. Signals help us to mark out the territory here: the single post to the rear of the train, and just past milepost 22 ¾, carries Dunford No. 2's Down Starter with No. 1's Down Distant beneath it. Notice, again, the two loops or "Goods Lines" flanking the Up and Down main. Through the summer haze in the background can be seen the faint outlines of the four stopblocks denoting the rear of the sidings at Dunford station on the Down side of the line.

H. Gordon Tidey

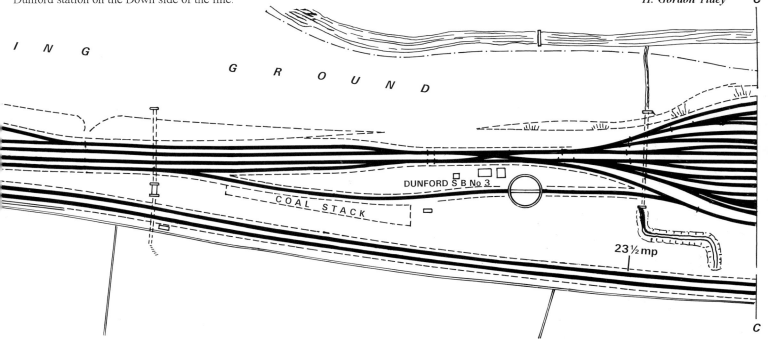

Approaches to Dunford Bridge, 1920's: No. **5426** *City of Chester* has cleared Dunford No. 2 signalbox, seen in the background, with a Down express; No. 2 signalbox was sited 1345 yards (just short of milepost 23 ¼) from No. 1 which stood on the Up platform. Just by the No. 2 box a "Pom Pom" is blowing off energetically at the entry to the reception sidings. The "Sam" is in lined green livery with a lettering style that lasted until around 1928. Three of the four coaches are 50'-0" Clerestory vehicles; the driver seems to be keeping something of a wary eye on the photographer! **H. Gordon Tidey**

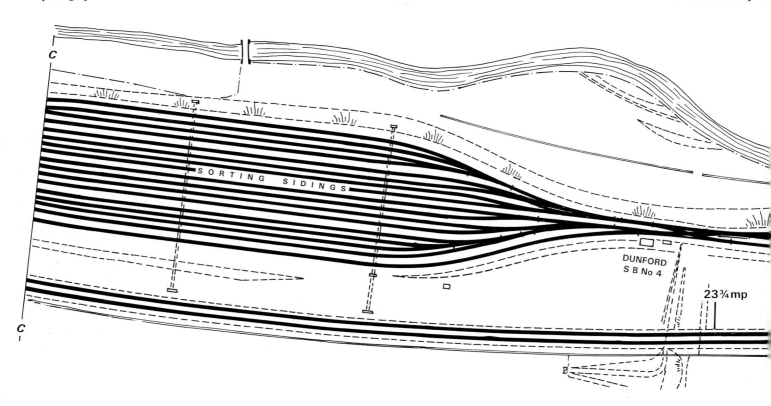

Dunford No. 2 Signalbox, looking east, March 26th 1950: This view looks towards the reception sidings, grouped into two pairs of two roads to each pair. The signalbox is a typical GCR pattern structure with characteristic fretted bargeboards and end window in the gable. Right to left the signals are:(1) Main line and Distant to Dunford No. 5 box; (2) Directive signal-Main and Up Goods to Dunford No. 5; (3) Signal and Distant, Loop to Dunford No. 5; (4) Dunford No. 2, Loop to Sidings; (5) Do. Loop to Sidings. This array of upper quadrant semaphores makes an interesting comparison with those of GCR pedigree which are just faintly discernible in the background to our view of "City of Chester". *R. E. Gee*

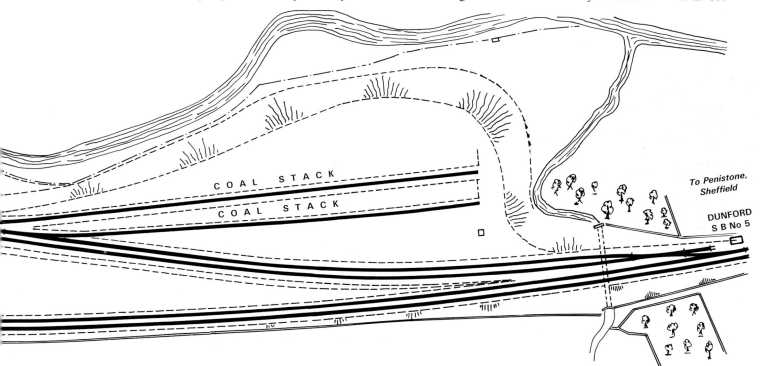

COAL STACK

COAL STACK

To Penistone, Sheffield

DUNFORD S B No 5

Dunford Bridge (Old Station, Prior To 1954)

From the earliest part of the twentieth century Dunford Bridge provided something of a focal point for freight operations on the eastern side of the Woodhead Tunnel. The station was opened, along with those at Penistone, Wortley, Deepcar, Oughty Bridge and Wadsley Bridge, in June 1845, prior to the opening of the eastern section of line from Sheffield (Bridgehouses) to Dunford itself. It will be remembered that the entire line from Manchester through to Sheffield did not open until December, 1845.

The station at Dunford Bridge, known locally and to all who worked there as just plain "Dunford", was sited on a gentle curve and was about 220 yards from the eastern portal of the Woodhead Tunnel. As at Woodhead station loops, or "Goods" lines had evolved on either side of the line to ease the flow of freight traffic. These ran east from the station: that on the Down line was commissioned on August 2nd 1896 and was almost ¾ mile long. The Up loop, lengthened in 1952, became over 1½ miles long and stretched as far as Dunford No. 2 signalbox (later Dunford East). No. 2 box controlled entry to the two pairs of reception sidings (four in all and some twenty chains in length) which handled traffic prior to its entry into the 16 sorting sidings. These sidings had been a focal point in the handling of east-bound coal empties at Dunford sice the early years of the century. Their main purpose was primarily to sort empty wagons, ensuring that they were returned to their rightful owners. This, of course, was long before the Nationalisation of the coal industry and at a time when most coal was still carried in wooden bodied (Private Owner) wagons.

Approval for the work had been given in 1899 at an estimated cost of £25,000; the sorting sidings were to be constructed by Messrs. Logan and Hemingway, a company heavily involved in the construction of the London Extension and in later projects into LNER days. A peculiarity of the work was that no record of tenders being invited or having been opened was found. The GCR minutes indicate that the contract was let on "a Schedule of Prices by negotiation." A Traffic Committee minute dated December 22nd 1899 records that work was to be postponed until compulsory powers were obtained for the land. Presumably, Messrs. Tinker, Coldwell, Greaves, Chapman and Col. W. T. W Spencer Stanhope - the local landowners - needed some persuasion! The GCR were determined to press on with this project as quickly as possible, despite all the subsequent wrangling over land purchase and rights of access. Delays were reported early on in 1900 and it was not until August 1st that an agreement was reached with Mr. Chapman, though the vendor reserved his ownership of the adjacent section of the river. Mr. Tinker was paid £1090 for his land, Mr. Bingley received £100 for access rights close to milepost 23¾ and Mr. Chapman got just £50 for a small parcel of land just short of milepost 24.

Contractor's Operations at Dunford began on October 4th and a report dated December 21st 1900 states that a "great deal of preparatory work has been done at Dunford Bridge." A completion date of August 1st 1900 was set, but a minute of late January reported that "works had not proceeded very rapidly."

Inclement weather, the holidays and the fact that Logan and Hemingway had not yet erected barracks (sic) for their men were blamed for the delay.

Delays to the new sidings were reported again in February - "very seriously impeded by the wintry weather" and... "a very wild and bleak location" are recorded. Even by July 19th 1901 the contractors were not as advanced as had been anticipated; a steam navvy had broken down and the Engineer was "making strong representations to them" (the company) Undaunted by all the obstacles that had arisen, Logan and Hemingway wrote to the GCR on November 6th Chief amongst the snags that delayed the project was the large and extensive drainage scheme that had to be put in hand when the excavations began. Tied in with this were the number of culverts that crossed the site - seven of these, some as large as six feet in diameter appear on the line plan. Vast quantities of rock had been found, in much bigger quantities than had been anticipated; this, coupled with the explanation that "Dunford Bridge is a very awkward, out of the way place to get men" were all part of Hemingway's plea to the company for more time - and money! By December 20th, the report states that Hemingway & Co. were "doing better" and by January 17th 1902, the whole of the earthworks in the Dunford Sorting Sidings was practically complete, "A further amount of permanent way has been laid." Further bad weather delayed matters in the latter part of January. Part of the sidings had been brought into use on December 1st 1901; the whole of the complex though, was not completed until March 24th 1902. Extensions to the sidings were approved on October 13th 1903 at an estimated cost of £4,922. Such was the unpredictablity of the wild Pennines their weather, geological formation and outlandish location.

To aid study and to help put the east - bound freight traffic into context, a sample from a 1920's working timetable is appended. This specimen, from September 1928, shows the yard in full operation with over 100 freight trains in a 24 hour period either passing through Dunford Bridge or stopping there for purposes of attaching or detaching wagons and re - marshalling The timetable shows a Pilot engine booked at Dunford from 8.00p.m. to 4.00a.m. Monday to Friday, suspended on Saturdays.

Prior to 1901 the freight operations here were more of a local nature. An MS&L line survey dated 1884 shows a group of four sidings on the Down line, just to the east of the station and two sidings on the Up side, with a shunting neck at either end These Up sidings are labelled as a stone depot, complete with their own stable, on the survey; they backed on to the banks of the River Dun (sic) which ran its course alongside the railway here The later plethora of signalboxes at Dunford would have come with the opening of the sorting sidings. Prior to this, two signalboxes sufficed; one on the Up station platform-up against the Windleden Lane overbridge and another, "Dunford East" (not to be confused with the later re-named No. 2 box), sited almost exactly halfway bewteen mileposts 22½ and 22¾ on the Up side of the line and controlling the exit from the stone depot.

East of Dunford Bridge, April 19th. 1954: Leaving Dunford Bridge the line continued to fall at 1-in-150 towards Hazlehead. B1 No. **61327** heads past the reception sidings with a 10-coach express towards Dunford No. 2, cutting through a landscape of open moors where windswept trees stand alone and dry stone walling appears to be the only visible marker between the wild countryside and the railway.   *B. K. B. Green*

London & North Eastern Railway(Great Central Section)

Passage and arrival of Up freight trains at Dunford/Dunford Sidings in a 24 our period. From "The Working Time Tables" of Passenger, Goods, Coal, Cattle, & c., trains. No. 1 section (west to east) Manchester & Cleethorpes (Main Line). No. 341 dated Monday, September 24th 1928, and until further notice.

1) Class B Goods to Marshgate (Doncaster) Mondays excepted. Dep.Godley Junction 12.10 a.m. Arr. Dunford 1.27. Dep. 3.10.

2) Class A Goods 9.00 pm. Brunswick (Liverpool) to Leeds Mondays excepted. Dep. Godley Junction 12.20 am. Pass Dunford 1.35.

3) Class A Goods 12.15 ex Ashton Moss Mondays excepted. Pass Dunford 2.38.

4) Class A Goods 11.42 Deansgate (Manchester) to Colwick Mondays excepted. Arr.Dunford 2.02. Dep. 3.40.

5) Class B Goods to Nottingham Mondays excepted. Dep. Dewsnap Sidings 12.50. Arr. Dunford No. 2 - 2.22. Dep. 2.30.

6) Class A Goods Ardwick to Grimsby. Mondays only. Dep.Ardwick yard 12.45. Pass Dunford 3.05.

7) Class A Cattle Birkenhead to Foss Islands (York). Mondays only. Dep. Godley Junction 1.45. Pass Dunford 2.38.

8) Class B Goods Mondays excepted. Dep. Godley Junction 2.15. Arr. Dunford. 3.17. Dep. 4.50.

9) Class B Goods Mondays only. ep.Dewsnap Sidings 2.05. Dunford pass 3.34.

10) Class C. 2.05 empties Ashton Moss to Wath. Mondays excepted. Dunford pass 3.41.

11) Class A Goods to Hull. Mondays only. Dep.Dewsnap Sidings 2.35. Dunford pass 4.08.

12) Class B Goods to Barnsley. Mondays only. Dep. from Dunford at 4.00.

13) Class B Goods to Dringhouses. Mondays only. Dep.Dewsnap Sidings. Arr. Dunford 4.14. Dep. 5.15.

14) Class B goods to Leeds. Mondays only. Dep.Dewsnap Sidings 3.05.Arr. Dunford. 4.26. Dep. 6.10.

15) Class B goods to Rotherham. Mondays excepted. Dep. from Dunford at 5.25.

16) Class B goods to Rotherham. Mondays only. Dep. Dewsnap Sidings 3.10. Arr. Dunford 4.40. Dep. 6.57.

17) Class B goods to Annesley. Mondays excepted. Dep.Ardwick yard 3.05. Arr. Dunford 4.42. Dep. 7.15.

18) Class C empties to Cudworth. Mondays excepted. Dep. Dewsnap Sidings 3.40. Dunford pass 3.42.

19) Class C empties to Wath yard. Mondays only. Dewsnap Sidings 3.45. Arr. Dunford 4.54. Dep. 5.06.

20) Class C empties to Warsop Junction. Dep.Dewsnap Sidings 4.10. Arr. Dunford 5.24. Dep. 7.30.

21) Class C empties (destination not marked). Dewsnap Sidings Dep.4.00. Dunford pass 3.44.

22) Class C empties to Mansfield (C. Sidings). Dewsnap sidings Dep. 4.25. Dunford pass 5.48.

23) Class C goods to Annesley. Mondays only. Dewsnap sidings Dep. 4.40. Dunford pass 6.02.

24) Class C goods to Annesley. Mondays & Saturdays excepted. Dep. Dewsnap Sidings 4.40. Dunford pass 6.02. (This train had a booked stop at Crowden for water. Its Mondays only counterpart did not).

25) Class C empties to Wath Yard. Dep. Ardwick yard 4.20. Arr. Dunford 6.20. Dep. 7.45.

26) Class B goods to Lincoln. Dep.Ardwick yard 4.00. Dunford pass 6.46.

27) Class B goods to Dringhouses. Dep. Dewsnap sidings 5.55. Arr. Dunford 7.20. Dep. 8.20.

28) Class C empties to Hickleton. Dewsnap sidings dep. 6.10. Dunford pass 7.30.

29) Class B goods. Dep. Glossop Central 6.55. Arr. Dunford 7.48. Dep. 8.35.

continued on page 160.....................................

continued from page 159..............................

30) *Class B goods to Ardsley. Godley Junction dep. 6.55. Arr. Dunford 8.08. Dep. 9.45. (Note that this train terminated at Dunford on Saturdays only).*

31) *Class C empties to Warsop Junction. Dewsnap sidings dep. 7.10. Arr. Dunford 8.36. Dep. 10.00.*

32) *Class C empties to Worksop. Dep. Ashton Moss sidings 7.12. Arr. Dunford 8.50. Dep. 10.48.*

33) *Class C Mineral working - as required. Dep. Dunford 11.10.*

34) *Class C empties to Mitchells Main. Mondays excepted. Dewsnap Sidings dep. 8.50. Arr. Dunford 10.06. Dep. 10.22.*

35) *Class C empties Ashton Moss sidings to Wath. Mondays only. Dep. from Ashton Moss 8.40. Arr. Dunford 10.06. Dep. 10.22.*

36) *Class C goods to Staveley Town. Saturdays only. Dep. Godley Junction 9.10. Arr. Dunford 10.37. Dep. 11.35.*

37) *Class C goods to Staveley Town. Saturdays excepted. Timings as previous the Saturday train was shunted at Deepcar.*

38) *Class B goods to Hull (Hessle Junction). Dewsnap Sdgs dep. 9.05. Dunford pass 10.57.*

39) *Class D goods. Dewsnap Sidings dep. 7.15 and shunted at all stations en route. Dunford (terminated) 6.32 p.m.*

40) *Class C empties to Wath Yard. Dep. Ashburys Yard 9.35. Arr. Dunford 11.16. Dep. 12.25.*

41) *Class B goods to Frodingham. Dewsnap Sidings dep. 102.5. Arr. Dunford 11.41. Dep. 1.30.*

42) *Fruit empties to Lincoln. Mondays excepted. Dep. Ardwick Yard 10.05. Dunford pass 11.52.*

43) *Class C empties. Dep. Dewsnap Sidings 11.05. Dunford pass 12.25.*

44) *Class C empties to Annesley. Dep. Godley Jcn 11.25. Arr. Dunford 12.43. Dep. 1.55.*

45) *Class C empties to Staveley Town. Dep. Dewsnap Sidings 11.45. arr. Dunford 1.16. Dep. 3.15.*

46) *Express Meat. 11.00 ex Huskisson (Liverpool) to London. Runs as required. Dunford pass 1.35.*

47) *Class C empties to Cudworth. Dep. Dewsnap Sidings 1.00. Dunford pass 2.21.*

48) *Class D goods. Dep. Dunford station 1.30. Return of 8.10 a.m. ex Barnsley Jcn.*

49) *Class C goods. Mondays excepted. 11.30 a.m. empties Heaton Mersey to Wath Yard. Dep. Godley Junction 12.40. Arr. Dunford 1.53. Dep. 3.20.*

50) *Class C empties to Wath Yard. Mondays only. Dep. Dewsnap sidings 12.40. Arr. Dunford 1.53. Dep. 3.20.*

51) *Class C empties. Saturdays excepted. Dep. Ardwick Yard 12.35. Arr. Dunford 2.11. Dep. 4.07.*

52) *Class C empties for Wath Yard. Dep. Ashton Moss 1.30. Dunford pass 3.25.*

53) *Class C empties Saturdays only. Dep. Ardwick Yard 12.53. Arr. Dunford 2.39. Dep. 4.07.*

54) *Class C empties to Wath Yard. Dep. Dewsnap Sidings 2.30. Dunford pass 4.17.*

55) *Fruit empties to Lincoln. Mondays excepted. Dep. Ardwick yard 2.20. Dunford pass 4.43.*

56) *Class B goods. Dep. Dunford 5.00. (Return of 8.10 a.m. ex Grimsby).*

57) *Class C empties to Warsop Junction. Saturdays excepted. Dep. Ardwick yard 2.15. Arr. Dunford 5.12. Dep. 6.30.*

58) *Do. above but Saturdays only. This train was booked to arrive at Bridgehouses goods depot 5 minutes later, at 7.27.*

59) *1.45 p.m. Perishable Huskisson to York. Saturdays only and runs when required. Dep. Godley Junction 4.07. Dunford pass 5.07. NOTE: When required, this train ran through to Glasgow; it was worked through to York by a GC section engine and guard. A load of 40 wagons was assisted from Stockport.*

60) *Class B goods. Sats. excepted. Dep. Ardwick yard 2.35. Arr. Dunford 5.24. Dep. 5.45.*

61) *Class C empties to Wath yard. Dewsnap Sidings dep. 4.20. Arr. Dunford 5.57. Dep. 6.10. On Saturdays only, this train was booked to pass Dunford at 6.09.*

62) *Class C goods. Dep. Dunford 6.40.*

63) *Class C empties Halewood to Grimethorpe. Runs when required. Mondays excepted. Godley Junction Dep. 4.40. Dunford pass 6.19.*

64) *Express Cattle ex Cross Lane (Salford). Tuesdays only). Pass Manchester London Road 3.02 (over South Junction line). Dunford pass 6.29.*

65) *Class C empties to Wath yard. Godley Junction dep. 5.33. Arr. Dunford 6.47. Dep. 8.25.*

66) *Express Meat. 3.10 Huskisson to Dringhouses. (Saturdays only). Dep. Godley Junction 5.35. Dunford pass 6.25.*

67) *Class C goods. Saturdays only. Dep. Dunford 6.50.*

68) *Class B goods to Lincoln. Saturdays only. Dep. Ardwick yard 4.25. Dunford pass 7.07.*

69) *Class D empties to Bentley Junction. Saturdays excepted. Dep. Dewsnap Sidings 5.35. Dunford pass 6.57.*

70) *Class B goods to Bentley Junction. Saturdays excepted. Dep. Godley Junction 6.00. Arr. Dunford 7.15. Dep. 10.00.*

71) *Class A goods to Bentley Junction. Sats only. (Called at Glossop to detach livestock as necessary). Arr. Dunford 7.22. Dep. 10.00.*

72) *Class B goods. Sats. excepted. Dewsnap sidings dep. 6.10. Dunford sidings 7.29.*

73) *Class A goods to Neasden. Saturdays only. Dep. Manchester London Road (Goods) 5.30. Dep. Dunford sidings 7.56.*

74) *5.25 Express Meat Huskisson to York. Saturdays excepted. Godley Junction dep. 7.18. Dunford pass 8.02.*

75) Class A Goods Deansgate (6.20 dep.) to Colwick. Saturdays only. Dunford pass 8.30.

76) *Goods Deansgate (6.50 dep.) to Colwick. Saturdays excepted. Dunford pass 8.30.*

77) *Class B Goods (Deansgate 5.20 dep.) to Dringhouses. Saturdays only. Arr. Dunford 9.03. Dep. 9.30.*

78) *Class A Goods to Lincoln. Dep. Manchester London Road (Goods) 6.45. Saturdays excepted. Dunford pass 8.42.*

79) *6.10 Express Meat Huskisson to Dringhouses. Saturdays excepted. Godley Junction dep. 8.08. Dunford pass 8.52.*

80) *Class A Goods 4.30 p.m. Brunswick to Leicester. Saturdays only. Godley Junction dep. 7.55. Dunford arr. 8.48. Dep. 10.25.*

81) *Class B Goods to Woodford. Saturdays only. Dewsnap Sidings dep. 8.00. Arr. Dunford 9.32. Dep. 10.20.*

82) *Express Goods to London. Saturdays excepted. Dep. Manchester London Road (Goods) 7.50. Dunford pass 9.23.*

83) *Class A goods (Deansgate 7.50 dep) to Peterborough. Saturdays only. Dunford pass 9.40.*

84) *Class B goods to Langwith Junction. Saturdays only. Dep. Ardwick Yard 8.00. Arr. Dunford 9.58. Dep. 10.30.*

85) *Class A goods to Dringhouses. Saturdays excepted. Dep. Ardwick Yard 7.55. Arr. Dunford 9.55. Dep. 11.35.*

86) *Express Goods 5.00 Huskisson to King's Cross. Saturdays excepted. Godley Junction pass 9.20. Dunford pass 10.10.*

87) *Class B goods to Hull. Saturdays only. Godley Junction dep. 9.32. Arr. Dunford 10.34. Dep. 12.35.*

88) *Express Goods to London. Saturdays excepted. Dep. Dewsnap sidings 9.15. Dunford pass 10.26. TIMETABLE NOTE: Load 35 wagons to Barnsley Junction, 40 forward increased by 5 wagons when worked by a four cylinder engine from Sheffield. No. 3 lights.*

89) *Class A goods to London. Dep. Manchester London Road (Goods) 9.05. Dunford pass 10.42.*

90) *8.00 Goods Denasgate to Leeds. Saturdays only. Dep. Godley Junction 9.52. Arr. Dunford 10.48. Dep. 11.30.*

91) *Class A Goods to York North Junction. Saturdays only. Dep. Dewsnap sidings 9.25 Dunford pass 10.57.*

92) *5.00 Express Goods Huskisson to King's Cross. Saturdays only. Dep. Godley Junction 9.25. Dunford pass 10.15.*

93) *Class A Goods 7.00 Brunswick to Nottingham. Saturdays excepted. Dep. Godley Junction 10.12. Dunford arr. 11.05. Dep. 1.25.*

94) *9.30 Express Goods Deansgate to Colwick. Saturdays excepted. Pass Godley Junction 10.22. Dunford pass 11.39.*

95) *Class A Goods to Lincoln. Saturdays only. Dep. Dewsnap sidings 10.30. Dunford pass 11.50.*

96) *7.50 Class A Goods Trafford Park to Lincoln. Saturdays excepted. Dep. Dewsnap sidings 10.30. Dunford pass 12.03.*

97) *Class A Goods to Leicester. Saturdays excepted. Dep. Dewsnap sidings 10.15. Dunford pass 11.51.*

98) *9.50 Class A Goods Trafford Park to Rotherham. Saturdays excepted. Godley Junction pass 11.12. Arr. Dunford 12.18. Dep. 3.00.*

99) *10.35 Class A Goods Deansgate to Leeds. Saturdays excepted. Godley Junction pass 11.35. Dunford pass 12.27.*

100) *Class B Goods 8.00 Brunswick to Ardsley. Sarturdays only. Godley Junction dep. 11.20. Dunford pass 12.18.*

101) *Class B Goods to Mansfield. Saturdays excepted. Dep. Manchester London Road (Goods) 10.20. Arr. Dunford 12.46. Dep. 2.50.*

102) *Class A Goods to Grimsby. Saturdays excepted. Dep. Ardwick yard 11.20. Dunford pass 12.55.*

103) *Class B Goods to Leeds. Saturdays excepted. Dep. Dewsnap sidings 11.45. Arr. Dunford 1.13. Dep. 3.50.*

104) *Class A Goods to Hull. Saturdays excepted. Dep. Ardwick yard 11.35. Arr. Dunford 1.50. Dep. 2.30.*

NOTES FROM THE TIMETABLE: All freight trains were allowed 3 minutes recovery time Godley to Valehouse and 3 minutes Valehouse to Woodhead. Freight trains were booked for a water stop at either Crowden or Woodhead. Just one Up freight - the 7.50 p.m. express goods from London Road - called for water at Penistone, where 9 minutes were allowed. A booked time is not shown for Crowden, where the majority slaked their thirst. Between 8 and 15 minutes are shown for water stops at Woodhead. On an additional note, water was available at Dunford: one column at the exit of the goods line to the Down main, the other at the west end of the Down platform. Further east, other water columns were supplied at Dunford No. 2 box, at No. 3 box - where a 55 ft. turntable was located and at Dunford No. 4 box. All these would have been supplied by the massive water tank sited on the Down platform by the station buildings.

Hazlehead Station, June 18th 1949: Apart from Penistone, there must have been very little local traffic to be had from the intermediate stations east of Woodhead and running into Sheffield Victoria. Some two miles east of Dunford Bridge was Hazlehead which had opened on May 1st 1846 and had but a short life, closing on November 1st the following year. Under MS&L auspices the station re-opened as "Hazlehead Bridge" on November 1st 1850. This name was used in public timetables, although, oddly enough, the LNER working timetable refers to the place as plain "Hazlehead"; the "Bridge" suffix was not applied to the station nameboard or the signalbox in modern times. In this midsummer scene the station is approaching its centenary year and a degree of dereliction looks apparent. B1 No. **61228** storms through with a Down express which the photographer noted as containing a good proportion of LMS stock. Notice the wagons in the goods yard loaded with pre-fabricated steelwork for the impending overhead electrification. Hazlehead finally closed to passengers on March 6th 1950.
R. E. Gee

Hazlehead Station, c.1906: Photography was still enough of a novelty in the early years of the century to bring about the "stand to attention" poses seen" here. The Station Master, one of his staff and at least three ladies pose for the camera, doubtless a large wooden affair, which has caught them for posterity from the Up side of the line. Notice the low platform-a feature which survived here until modern times. ***Courtesy GCRS***

Hazlehead, June 18th 1949: Almost half a century has passed, the same station buildings stand and we are now into the second year of British Railways' ownership. Class O2 No **63981** passes through with a Down freight and by the looks of things this is another loaded coal train from the Yorkshire pits. An O4 passes by on the Up line. ***R.E.Gee***

Approaching Hazlehead, 19th April 1954: By way of a contrast to our other scenes, "Black 5" No **45276** approaches Hazlehead station with an Up Excursion working-W658, the two front coaches being of Great Western origin. Steam is having its last fling at through working over Woodhead, although the section of line from Wath to Dunford Bridge was officially inaugurated, under Stage 1, for electric traction (for all freight traffic) on February 4th. 1952. Notice Hazlehead's signalbox, perched high up on the cutting slope; an MS&L design, it makes an interesting companion to our view of the early box at Gorton Station which we saw in volume 1. ***B. K. B. Green***

As Britain recovered from the Second World War, the railways were busier than ever. A vast home-based manufacturing industry was getting back into gear to supply a world starved of goods. The imposition of fuel rationing, with few people owning cars anyway, meant a massive volume of traffic was moved by rail. The enthusiast who wanted to photograph trains, though, had to struggle with a paucity of film and paper, coupled with the fact that good cameras were very expensive by today's standards. Despite this, Doug Darby and his colleagues were able to record for posterity these splendid scenes reproduced here-all steam and barely a trace of the long-awaited electrification in sight-in the open countryside between Hazlehead and Penistone. The date is September 3rd 1949.

Almost perfect lighting and nice clean condition makes Gorton B1 No. **61161** look every inch the part as she comes up the 1-in-124 towards Hazlehead at the head of the 10.00 am Marylebone to Manchester express (2.04 ex Sheffield). The coaching stock is almost totally traditional LNER stock. Only a Thompson steel-sided carriage, the second vehicle, interrupts the otherwise uniform appearance.

Let the sun shine and just sit back and watch the trains! Steam, steam and more steam was there for the taking; only the newly-erected concrete posts for the 33kV electric feeder cable give any indication of the impending changes in traction. 04/7 No. **63669**, a Robinson 2-8-0 rebuilt by Gresley with a variation of the O2 boiler, comes up the bank with a through freight conveying, mostly, coal in wooden-bodied wagons. Disappearing along the Up line, yet another freight train heads east

Both: J. D. Darby

Between Hazlehead and Penistone

Approaching Hazlehead from Bullhouse, September 3rd 1949: A scene some ¼ of a mile east of Hazlehead station. Pictures showing clear views of entire trains are not that common-especially on the Woodhead line. This lovely late summer scene, complete with harvested stooks and striding farmer, depicts a Skegness to Manchester train double-headed, somewhat unusually, by an N5 No. **69245** and a K3 No. **61960**. Heading in the opposite direction is an amazing sight-an ensemble of no less than five locomotives, with J39 No. **4757** bringing up the rear, trotting downhill towards Sheffield. In steam days here such sights were, apparently, quite common. The dearth of freight traffic at weekend would leave an imbalance of engines at the Manchester end of the line; hence the need to return engines, typically to sheds such as Mexborough, as seen here. A final comment on the Down train is worth making: what an amazing variety of coaching stock! Amongst the 11 vehicles can be seen Great Central, LNER, Great Western and LMS coaches. Something of a contrast to the totally predictable make-up of today's Trans-Pennine expresses.   *J. D. Darby*

September 3rd 1949: 04/3 No. **63812** comes up the bank with a through freight. In contrast to the scenes showing the mass tanshipment of coal, this train has at least six wagon loads of what appears to be bulk strapped timber mingled amongst the wooden-bodied coal wagons. The fireman stands erect looking somewhat apprehensively at the photographer. ***J. D. Darby***

June 18th 1949: As a change from a Robinson 2-8-0 we look at a Gresley design, one of the 3-cylinder LNER class 02 mineral engines which the celebrated designer had introduced to the Great Northern in 1917. No. **63984**, then allocated to Langwith, passes at the head of a Down coal train-the lifeblood of Woodhead. Owing to the curvature of the line here, it is not possible to ascertain whether or not the train is being banked.   *R. E. Gee*

In steam days, coal trains originating from the various Yorkshire pits and bound westward via Woodhead were faced with a series of uphill slogs in the first few miles of their journeys. En route from Wath yard, the notorious Wentworth bank, some two miles on a gradient of 1-in-40, required both double headed motive power and double banking in the rear. The famous, or perhaps infamous Garratt, helped out here in latter years. Heading westwards on the main line from Barnsley Junction, Penistone, banking was required almost to the mouth of the Woodhead Tunnel. Prior to the construction of the new tunnel, the rising gradient, which varied from 1 in 100 just past Barnsley Junction to 1 in 135 through Dunford Bridge station, changed to a downhil

1 in 493 just a few yards beyond the station, then to a further downgrade of 1 in 201 through the tunnel itself. This enabled banking engines to be detached once clear of Dunford station, cross via the facing crossover between the station and the tunnel mouth before running back down the bank to Barnsley Junction again. Under rule 133, clearly stated in the 1947 LNER sectional appendix, trains requiring an engine to assist in the rear (except where specially authorised) had to be brought to a stand and the assisting engine had to be coupled to the train. Two photographs taken between Dunford Bridge and Hazlehead in the early years of British Railways show banking engines at work in typical fashion to that described.

September 3rd 1949: A Q4 0-8-0 in very grimy condition and carrying its pre-Nationalisation lettering and number - **3205**, provides a shove along the 1 in 135. The goods guard, impeccably attired in collar and tie (yes!) at the back of his 20-ton brake van, looks completely unperturbed by what must have been an exhilarating ride! Note the clean ballast and beautifully cared for permanent way.

June 18th 1949: Almost at the same spot, N5 0-6-2 tank, still lettered LNER and numbered **9348**, provides assistance at the rear of a westbound (Down) coal train.

Both photos; J. D. Darby

The Hepworth Iron Company

Just west of the site of Hazlehead station was the 1½ mile branch to the Hepworth Iron Company's works. Hepworth Iron was formed in 1858 and the branch was built at the same time. The initial section of the single line branch was steeply graded and, originally, traffic was hauled up the incline by a stationary winding engine. In a manner similar to the use of such things elsewhere, the stationary engine was replaced by a locomotive. The first of these was named *Polly*; a second engine, *Ebor* was added afterwards. In 1960, when an RCTS Railtour visited the works, two 0-6-0 tank locomotives were in use: *Hepworth* - built by the Yorkshire Engine Company at their Meadow Hall works in Sheffield in 1905. *Ebor* - built by Hudswell Clarke in 1899 for the Barry Railway and ran as No. 33. After the Barry was amalgamated into the GWR, the engine was renumbered 781. In this guise she ran until 1932 when she was sold to Robert Stephenson & Co. A year later the erstwhile No. 781 was bought by Hepworth Iron and was named *Ebor* using her predecessor's nameplates.

(Top) On an RCTS Railtour of April 9th 1960, *Hepworth* is seen at Crow Edge, just over a mile north of the junction with the GCR main line. The sight of several dozen enthusiasts packed into five loose-coupled open wagons would, no doubt, bring hasty condemnation from the HSE today   *B. Hilton*

(Centre) 1952 - a view looking north through the narrow confines of the ¼ mile - long tunnel which took the branch up towards and under the B6106 Holmfirth to Penistone road. An oddly named thoroughfare -"Mucky Lane" connected with the road and paralleled the tunnel as far as Crow Edge Slack where a number of collieries were found. One of these, Sledbrook Colliery, was once served by the railway, though it is not known when the coal workings at this pit were exhausted. By the looks of the ground on top of the railway the tunnel may well have been built on the "cut and cover" principle; the possible objective being to keep this section of the branch clear of snow, no mean feat on land having a mean altitude of around 900 feet above sea-level.

David Ibbotson

(Bottom) April 9th 1960, *Hepworth* stands at the branch Home signal at the Hazlehead end of the line. Notice the overhead catenary denoting the limits of electrification off the main line.   ***Brian Hilton***

Bullhouse

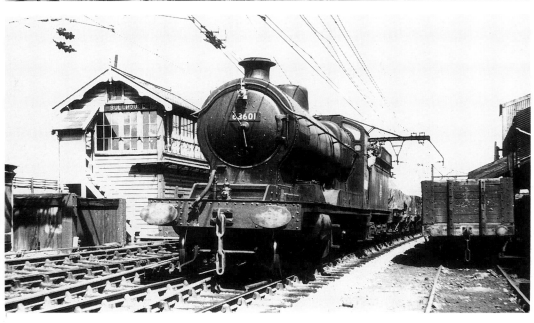

(Above) Near Bullhouse, June 3rd. 1950: Straying far from its native heath, former North Eastern Railway 0-8-0, LNER Class Q6 No. **63387**, has cleared the overbridge carrying Liley Lane over the main and goods lines. This bridge was numbered 81 in the LNER register and was known locally as "Ecklands". Behind the train, Shore Hall Lane level crossing has been cleared and the train, a mixed freight, is heading in the direction of the colliery at Bullhouse. Today, the site here is almost unrecognisable as a railway, a thicket of trees covers the ground where the photographer stands. Some solace can be taken, though, in the use of the alignment as part of the "Upper Don Trail" which has become a well used route for walkers, bikers and joggers. ***Ken Boulter***

(Centre) Bullhouse, April 19th. 1954: With the overhead catenary erect and fully wired, steam is having its last fling with through workings. B1 No. **61162** heads the 10.05 Nottingham to Liverpool relief train with ten coaches behind the tender on the approach to Bullhouse Colliery. Notice the pointwork in the foreground: it was here that the Down goods loop from Thurlstone ended-a facility brought into use on July 30th, 1900. ***B. K. B. Green***

Bullhouse Colliery Sidings, n.d: A striking view of O4 No **63601** passing with a Down freight. The signalbox, of wooden construction to a standard Great Central design, was located at 1 mile, 648 yards east of Hazelhead box. ***Kenneth Field***

Now approaching Penistone, trains clear of Hazlehead and Bullhouse colliery approached the crossing at Thurlstone. The signalbox here controlled entry to the previously mentioned Down loop as well as acting as a block post and watching over the gated crossing.

Thurlstone, Down loop, April 19th 1954: 02 No. **63969** and its train have been put "inside" and the engine steams hard along the Down loop (referred to by the LNER incidentally as the "Down Goods Independent") in the direction of Bullhouse. The train carries Class "C" lights indicating a through freight working. The first four wagons are covered by tarpaulins; immediately behind these a well wagon carries what appears to be large timber roof trusses. All revenue earning mixed freight and symbolizing the sort of traffic that departed from the railways long ago.

B. K. B Green

Thurlstone, April 6th 1953: Moving some 200 yards or so nearer to Penistone and a scene taken a year or so earlier. A rather unusual combination of motive power is seen as J11 No. **64343** pilots LMS Class 4 2-6-0 No. **43114** with a Down excursion working (number M952) from Rotherham to Hyde Road (for Belle Vue, Manchester).

B. K. B. Green

Thurlstone Crossing, April 19th 1954: Though this picture has been seen before in another publication I make no apologies for giving it another airing here. In this magnificent view steam is having one of its last flings over Woodhead prior to full electrification later in 1954. B1 No. **61228** gives the rising gradient of 1-in-130 towards Dunford and the tunnel mouth its very best shot with a Down express. A fitting reminder of the thrilling sight of the steam locomotive in full flight and arguably one of the best steam action shots ever taken on this route. **B. K. B. Green**

Between Penistone and Thurlstone, May 19th 1947: This was the scene looking westwards from the overbridge where Penistone Goods was located. Drifting down from Thurlstone Crossing is 04/4 No. **3907**. The engine, a rebuild of one of Robinson's large boilered 2-8-0's (Class 8M), is at the head of a Class B freight train. No. 3907's parentage can be discerned by the larger spectacle plate forming the front of the cab. Notice the signals: barely ¾ mile separated Penistone Goods box from that at Thurlstone Crossing - notice the use of a "slotted" Distant arm for the latter. Notice, too, the fogman's hut to the right of the locomotive on the Up line; the lever outside the little cabin actuated a detonator placer for the Distant signal ahead. Spare a thought for the poor souls who must have stood for hours on end in murky and freezing conditions to ensure the safe passage of trains over such a densely trafficked route. **W. Hudson collection**

Scenes at Penistone Goods, n.d:

(Upper) A picture of great interest, showing as it does something of the site surrounding the original Penistone station which had opened in July 1845. In 1869 Sir Edward Watkin is said to have directed that the future station at Penistone should be situated where the Huddersfield branch of the L&Y joined the MS&L main line. This picture looks east towards the structure carrying the railway over Bridge Street. Visible to the right in the distance are the goods facilities here which took over the site of the original Penistone passenger station. The goods shed can be faintly made out; beyond this was an office, a stable and coal "shoots" (drops). Penistone, new, station opened on February 1st 1874. The signalbox, Penistone Goods, controlled the up and down loops and crossover, part of a package of alterations at Penistone dating from November 1899. Passing through is an unidentified B1 at the head of an Up passenger train. A tank engine, probably an N5, blows off impatiently in the Down loop beyond the signalbox.

(Centre) Certainly not a picture of the highest quality by any means, but one, nevertheless, worthy of sharing. This time the photographer has moved from his overbridge perch down to rail-level to catch an original "Director" (D10) and a B5 4-6-0 running into Penistone with an Up express. The 4-4-0 has the plain wartime "NE" initials on the tender, but it is not possible to discern the number on the cabside.

(Lower) From a similar viewpoint to the previous picture, a clearer glimpse of operations shows a J11 running past Penistone Goods signalbox with a local, possibly a "Trip" or "pilot" freight. The "Pom-Pom" has received its 1946 number via white stencilled numbers on the cabside, a practice reportedly carried out at local level at the various running sheds.

(All)Author's collection

Penistone

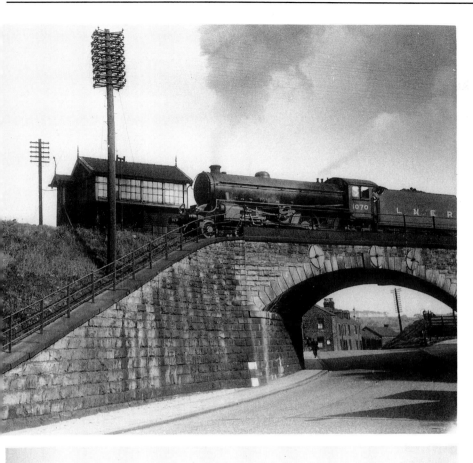

July 1st 1850-opening of Huddersfield branch.
November 1st 1855-opening of Barnsley branch.

Leaving Penistone, c.1947: The biggest change in motive power over the GC line after the Second War was the introduction of the Thompson B1s in the latter part of 1946. In this scene the camera is pointed at the overbridge taking the railway westbound from Penistone station over Church Street and the junction with Station Road - seen off to the right. B1 No. **1070**, then a Gorton engine, storms away towards Manchester with a Down express past Penistone West signalbox. Glancing back along the train, the driver assures himself that all is well; unmoved by the sight and sound of such things, a lone figure saunters beyond the bridge along towards the Wentworth Arms and the cottages beyond. *Author's collection*

Penistone, view along Church Street looking west c.1946: The signpost on the gas lamp points sparse road traffic towards Huddersfield and Manchester, Jubb's Fisheries have closed for the day in an otherwise quiet afternoon cameo. Up on the railway a rousing scene is portrayed: A Down express pulls away from Penistone station - Starter and Distant are pegged off; the guard leans from the brake portion of a Gresley corridor third and Director No. **2667** *Somme* gives the train, cattle van included, a rousing shove in a westerly direction. How unremarkable the local populace must have thought all this was at the time. Yet to us it is a valuable little slice of history showing a true Great Central engine at work on a railway where steam was still king and would remain so for quite some years to come. *Author's collection*

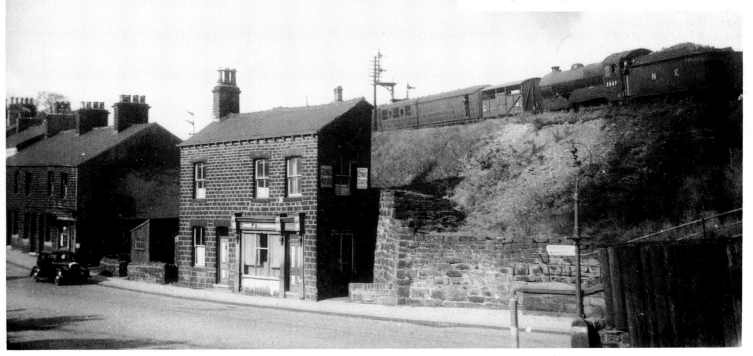

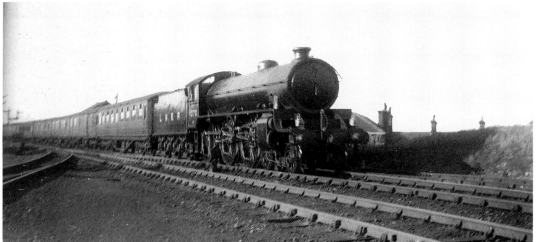

West end of Penistone Station

(Upper) c.1945: Though of indifferent technical quality , I felt this scene was worthy of inclusion on account of the sheer atmosphere it exudes. The photographer has walked along St. Mary's Street, past the Commercial Inn and the Cattle Market and paused by the bridge that carried the railway over Bridge Street. Gradually, the peace is disturbed by the sight and sound of a J39 banking a freight train in the rear up and along the 1-in-100/1-in-130 in the Down direction. The train has now cleared Penistone station and is about to pass Penistone Goods en route westwards towards Dunford Bridge via Thurlstone and Bullhouse. The J39 carries a number in the 27XX series-indicating one of the Darlington-built engines running in the pre-1946 era.

(Centre) c.late 1946: Brand New! B1 No. **1070** rolls in from Manchester with an Up express. The first batches of the new 4-6-0's appeared in black livery with single red lining. A peculiarity applied to the batch numbered 1040-1093 was the use of smaller (10" high) numbers on the cabside as opposed to 12" letters "LNER" on the tender. Such was the sparkling ensemble passing Penistone West box as the photographer, who had edged his way past the end of the island platform, opened his shutter to present us with this rather fine sight.

(Lower) c.1946/47: As seen elsewhere, new B1's were the order of the day over Woodhead in the early post-War years. On a seemingly wet and dismal day No. **1068** rolls in with an Up express. Prior to May, 1948 1068 was a Leeds, Neville Hill engine before migrating to the north-east where it spent the bulk of its career. The old order still reigns, though, on the Down line. The platform Starter is off as a B7 piloted by a Director pulls away in the direction of Manchester.

(All)Author's collection

Penistone, May 10th 1947: As can be witnessed from the photographic coverage in this book, B1 4-6-0's became the mainstay of express motive power on the Woodhead line from their introduction and gradual spread from 1943 onwards. As such, the Thompson LNER standard design formed an interregnum between the departure of the Gresley B17 and the GCR designs of Robinson and the later, all pervading, "Juice Engines". All the more surprising, then, that a B17 should appear by contrast at this late stage. A decidedly grubby No. **1669** *Barnsley,* then a Leciester engine, rolls into the station at the head of an Up express, possibly the 2.20 p.m. to Manchester London Road to Marylebone made up to eight or more coaches. This was due at Penistone at 3.15; arrival at London Marylebone was 7.15. An interesting social group poses on the platform: a lady takes a sideways look at the engine, a young man, his raincoat slung over his shoulder, stares over at the photographer, a waistcoated porter walks in front of him head inclined towards the ground. The platform hoarding proclaims "Brylcreem your hair" something taken to heart by the hatless character with the service-type jacket. Raincoats and Trilby hats seem *de rigeur* for the five characters on the right clutching at their leather briefcases; staring at the incoming train, doubtless they are wondering if they will get a seat. In an age when new cars were virtually unobtainable and second-hand ones fetched sky-high prices, many businessmen had little option but to travel by train. ***Author's collection***

Penistone Station, west end, May 18th 1948: A refreshing change from black B1s is provided by the welcome sight of a green member of the species-No. **1158** pulling away from Penistone with a Down express. 1158 was one of a batch of fifty B1's built by Vulcan Foundry in 1947. The engine entered traffic on May 14th of that year and was allocated to Gorton shed from new. When this photograph was taken her regular driver was Harry Sheppard, one of 20 men in the Gorton No. 1 Express Passenger link. In October 1953, prior to full electrification of the Woodhead line, 1158 was sent to Doncaster where it spent the rest of its days before withdrawal in April, 1966. ***K. H. Boulter***

Winter at Penistone, 1947

As mentioned already, the awful winter of 1947 played havoc with train services over Woodhead. Here, in those incredible conditions of over half a century ago, is first-hand testimony showing the scene during and after the snow clearance. Fierce controversy raged in the correspondence pages of The Railway Gazette in March 1947 over the merits of rotary versus V - front snow ploughs. One G. Richard Parkes, writing from Glasgow, was fiercely critical of the LNER for relying solely on the V-front (wedge) ploughs instead of using the rotary plough where snow is cut and thrown clear of the tracks. Parkes aroused the wrath of George Dow, then LNER Press Relations Officer, by claiming that no intelligent use had been made by the company of the V-shaped ploughs either.

Penistone 1947

(Above) A very wintry scene indeed at the west end of the station with the rail heads barely visible. Standing on the Down Main line steam roars from the safety valves of J39 No. **4740** as the fireman "puts the bag in" to top up the tender tank. Notice the tarpaulin placed over the top of the cattle wagon to afford a degree of extra protection for the poor beasts within. (Right) A Class O1 2-8-0, number unknown, struggles into the station past Penistone West box with an Up through train of vans. By the looks of things, this may well have been one of the first trains to be able to run through from Manchester on February 13th after snow clearance was effected.

(Both) Author's collection

(Above) **This was the LNER's snow-fighting weapon at this time:** two Robinson 2-8-0's are sandwiched between a brake van which acts as mess quarters for the operating staff. At either end of the ensemble converted ex - GCR tenders are fitted with the wedge-shaped (V-fronted) snow ploughs. With the rail heads just clear, the snow ploughs pass through the main line platforms from Huddersfield Junction.
(Below) **Penistone West's Down Main Home board is pegged off** as the snow-clearing force blasts its way westwards along the main line towards Penistone Goods and Thurlstone. *(Both) Author's collection*

An official visit by a British Rail photographer recorded a station in decline some twenty one months after regular main line passenger services had been withdrawn. However, the station buildings are still largely intact in this view looking towards Sheffield, the distinctive canopies continuing to serve their purpose, those on the Up side for both passengers gaining access to and from the Huddersfield line and railway departmental use. Redundant track on the Down side has by now been removed and protective fencing erected along the alignment of the erstwhile platform one.   **Sept. 1971**
Fastline Photographic

Penistone

The main buildings at **Penistone** were large and imposing without perhaps being impressive. **(Above)** Located at the top of a somewhat narrow approach adjoining Station Road, the buildings were hemmed in at the east end by the Huddersfield line platform, thus placing restrictions on the photographer. The view here reflects that difficulty, with long shadows effectively eliminating much of the detail. The Up (main line) platform canopy **(Right),** blanks out the light to the detriment of the building detail.

Fastline Photographic

(Above) Penistone, June 6th 1953. C13 No. **67434**, a Barnsley engine (36D), awaits departure with a local train for Barnsley (Court House), thought to be the 12.15pm Saturdays Only, calling at Silkstone, Dodworth, and Summer Lane *en route*. This local service, along with the remaining intermediate stations between Penistone and Sheffield, all succumbed to closure in July 1959. The locomotive was not quite so lucky, being withdrawn from service in August 1957, albeit having given over half a century of service.

A L Brown, courtesy N E Stead

(Right) Penistone, September 1971. Although the Manchester route (left) had by now lost its regular passenger trains, the air of dereliction that often engulfs redundant railway premises has not yet fully taken hold. Rationalisation, in the form of track removal on the Down side, and clearance of some station buildings from the Huddersfield line platforms however, gave the sign of things to come.

Fastline Photographic

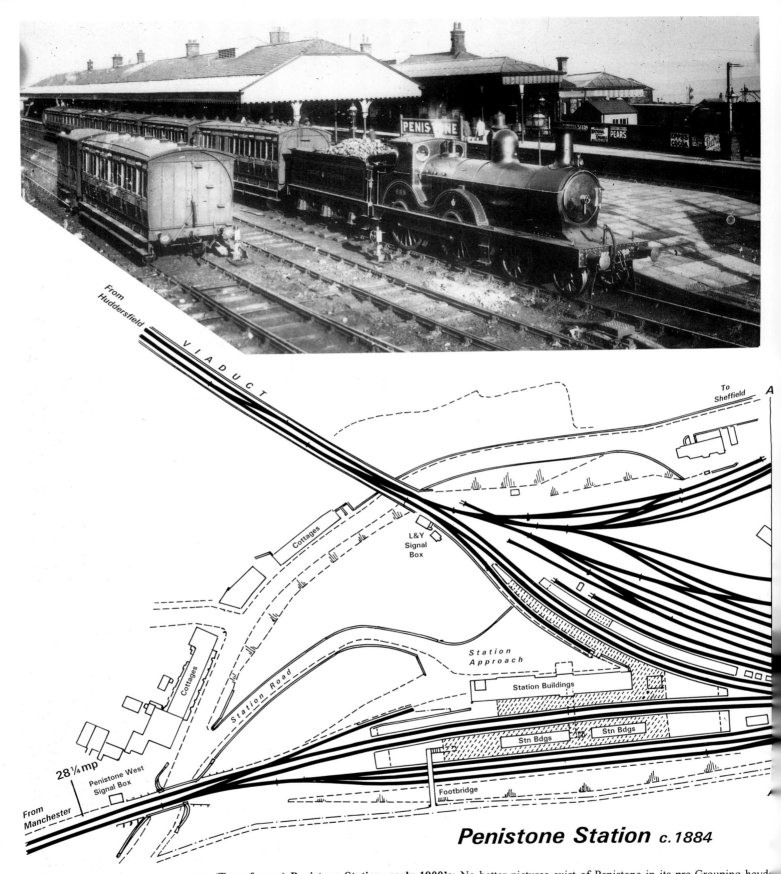

Penistone Station *c.1884*

From Huddersfield

VIADUCT

To Sheffield

Cottages

L&Y Signal Box

Cottages

Station Road

Station Approach

Station Buildings

Stn Bdgs

Stn Bdgs

28¼ mp

Penistone West Signal Box

From Manchester

Footbridge

(Top of page) Penistone Station, early 1900's: No better pictures exist of Penistone in its pre-Grouping heyda[y] than those taken by local photographer Biltcliffe & Son whose activities here existed until the 1950's. In this supe[rb] period view at the east end of the station, looking north, Parker Class 2A No. **689** waits at platform 1 with a train [of] six 6-wheelers-probably a stopping train from Manchester to Sheffield. The coaches appear in the two-tone brow[n] and French grey livery used until around the end of 1903. Across on the L&Y's side of the station two LNW[R] liveried coaches appear along with the shunting signals and loading gauge in the joint goods yard.

Penistone Station, looking east to Huddersfield and Barnsley Junctions, 1900s: This striking Biltcliffe photograph epitomises Edwardian Penistone with the Cammell Laird, formerly Charles Cammell & Co., steelworks dominating the scene; the whole panorama suiting admirably the well-worn phrase "a hive of activity." Steel and coal were what South Yorkshire was about, the latter well illustrated by the activities of the Worsborough Branch mentioned elsewhere. At platform 1 ....*continued below*

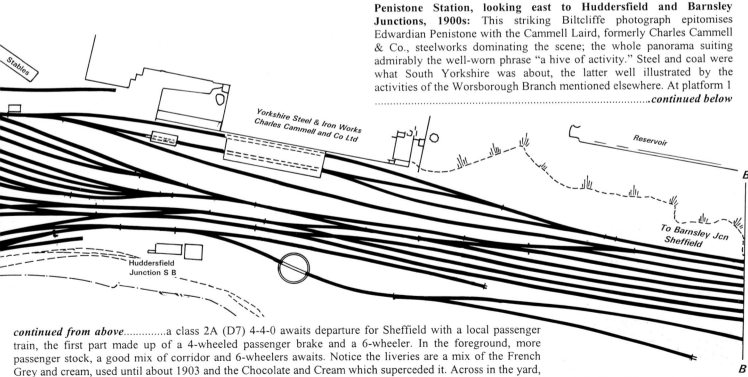

***continued from above*.............a class 2A (D7) 4-4-0 awaits departure for Sheffield with a local passenger train, the first part made up of a 4-wheeled passenger brake and a 6-wheeler. In the foreground, more passenger stock, a good mix of corridor and 6-wheelers awaits. Notice the liveries are a mix of the French Grey and cream, used until about 1903 and the Chocolate and Cream which superceded it. Across in the yard, a plethora of loaded coal wagons await transit: Shireoaks, J&W.Tomlinson, S.J.Claye and MR ownership being noted. Absent is any sign of L&Y vehicles; but perhaps a reminder is needed that this was, in fact, joint territory. Under an agreement dated September 28th 1871, the L&Y paid the MS&L £200 per annum for the use of Penistone station. Expenses were apportioned according to the number of passengers of each company. One third was charged on through traffic and two thirds on each company's bookings at or to Penistone station. Certainly, much goods traffic was generated by Cammell Laird who rebuilt the steelworks at a later date; by 1910 the whole frontage seen here had been radically altered. However, the troubles of the later 1920s and early 1930s saw a drastic reduction of their operations here. Future rationalisation and eventual closure of the steelworks ensured that the area seen here was to become little more than a wasteland.

Biltcliffe & Sons

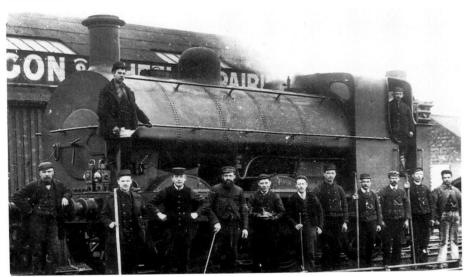

(Above) Penistone Station, n.d: The photographer has gone off station limits to give us this view of the joint L&Y/MS&L station. The MS&L, though, owned the lion's share of the land surrounding the station. Opened in 1874, the station sat in the fork of the MS&L main line and the L&Y's line to Huddersfield. The latter can be seen here branching away to the right; an LMS brake 3rd. can be seen at the rear of a train standing in the branch platform, notice the adjoining "waiting shelter." Looking away in an opposite direction the Penistone West Down Home is pegged "off"; just two passengers appear to be waiting at platform 2. On the south side of this island platform were three siding roads forming an effective loop between Huddersfield Junction and Penistone West boxes. The branch Home signal has a slotted concrete post, a feature used by the LNER. On the right, the lines seen formed part of a group of sidings which stood adjacent to the works of Messrs. Charles Cammell (later Cammell Laird). *Author's collection*

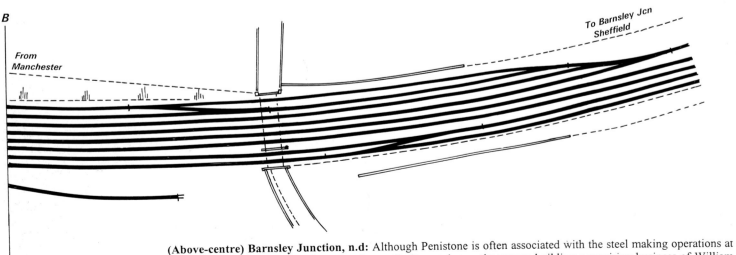

(Above-centre) Barnsley Junction, n.d: Although Penistone is often associated with the steel making operations at Cammell Laird, other industries existed as well. One such was the wagon building a repairing business of William Gittus. The company's small shops were situated by milepost 29 just across from Barnsley Junction signalbox and close by the Penistone to Sheffield Road. Thirteen men pose in front of Gittus's workshops; the engine is a Sacre "Humpie" 0-6-0 Saddle tank, a class built by him from 1871 and later modified by Robinson. *courtesy David Green*

Huddersfield Junction

(Above) The lofty signalbox, mounted on massive timber supports, dominates this scene as a double-headed express with J11, possibly No. **5231** as the pilot engine, enters the station from the Sheffield direction. The photograph is taken from the north-west end of the island platform which stood in the fork between the main line and the Huddersfield branch; the latter runs off to the left. The distinctive signalbox dated from around 1887 when extensive re-modelling of the junction and its adjacent lines took place.

(Centre) With steam leaking in copious quantities and looking very much down-at-heel, an unidentified N5 tank engine ambles over the junction with a Down pick-up freight.
(both circa 1945/46)
Author's collection

Huddersfield Junction, c.1945: An unidentified O4 crosses the junction with a mixed Down freight. All the "pegs" are off giving the driver a clear run through Penistone station and towards Penistone West and Penistone Goods boxes. *Author's collection*

Wellhouse Tunnel, June 5th 1954: The former L&Y line from Huddersfield to Penistone is full of interest, containing, amongst other things, no less than six tunnels. One of these is Wellhouse tunnel, situated between Denby Dale and Penistone itself. Emerging from the tunnel is B1 No. **61141** with a Bradford to Marylebone train-a special working and carrying the reporting number C904. Notice the slotted concrete post carrying the Distant signal.   *Ken Boulter*

Leaving Penistone for Huddersfield and Barnsley, in a northerly and easterly direction respectively, the two railways crossed the Don Valley by means of impressive viaducts. That belonging to the L&Y and taking their thirteen mile line to Huddersfield comprises twenty arches, each of 30 ft. span and carries the railway 98 ft. above the river. The viaduct is 1100 ft. long and the line is curved on a 40-chain radius. The branch was opened on July 1st 1850.

Looking north c.1947: A branch train from Huddersfield, drawn bunker-first by an ex-L&Y 2-4-2 tank, runs into Penistone station. The square signalbox, with its brick base and hipped roof was known as "Penistone North". Notice the check rail to cope with the sharply curved track; the line cutting in on the far left was a 4 ½ chain spur which ran round the back of the Huddersfield-bound platform. It was removed in later years. The corresponding line on the right led to the sidings jointly owned by the M&SL and the L&Y adjoining the Yorkshire Steel and Iron Works of Charles Cammell & Co. Ltd. (later Cammell Laird). A small group of sidings also existed on the north side of the steel works, adjacent to Penistone Grammar School.   *Author's collection*

Penistone Viaduct, April 23rd 1950: The viaduct is seen almost in its entirety; Penistone North's Home signal is off, while Huddersfield Junction's Distant beckons caution. A Class B1 (number unknown) slows over the viaduct with the diverted 10.25 a.m. Manchester to London Marylebone express. Today is a Sunday and engineering work has closed the Woodhead tunnels entirely. As a result, southbound expresses over the former GCR from Manchester have run to Huddersfield via Stalybridge and then the former LNWR route via Standedge. Reversal will have taken place in Huddersfield with a fresh engine attached in the rear. Working via Springwood Junction, Lockwood Viaduct and no less than six tunnels, the train has arrived back on its original route. What a wonderful diversion! The reverse procedure will apply to Down trains. *R. E. Gee*

Penistone Viaduct, April 6th 1953: The viaduct seen from its westerly aspect with the splendid open countryside of the Don Valley all around. Another B1, this time identified as No. **61061** heads into Penistone station with the Up "South Yorkshireman". This train was a Bradford to London Marylebone express which had first appeared in the post-War timetables in May 1948. The train left Bradford Exchange at 10.00 a.m. with conditional stops at Brockholes and Shepley on the section from Huddersfield. After reaching Sheffield at 11.27, "The South Yorkshireman" called at Nottingham, Loughborough, Leicester, Rugby and Aylesbury. Arrival in Marylebone was at 3.30 p.m. An oddity of the working was the omission of a stop at Penistone on the Up journey, but a call there on the return working to Bradford. *B. K. B. Green*

Penistone, c.1948. Huddersfield Junction is in full view and a nice clean B1, number unknown, pulls away, tender first, from the Huddersfield branch platform with an Up stopping train. The "pegs" are off for the Sheffield route and the train will have a clear run to Barnsley Junction, the site of which can be identified by the distant plume of steam to the right of the departing loco. The first coach is an ex-East Coast Joint Stock clerestory vehicle, but it has not been possible to fully decipher the number. The railwayman to the right of the picture could possibly be guarding the barrow crossing, but similarly seems oblivious to the photographer.

Authors collection

Huddersfield Junction, June 2nd 1966: This box and adjacent Barnsley Junction, were two of the largest signal box structures on the Woodhead line. Huddersfield Junction box dated from the late 1880's, the frame carrying 68 levers. The heavy timber supports were later supplanted by brick pillars. Surviving operationally until 1998, Huddersfield Junction, latterly renamed "Penistone", had singularly controlled what lines were left in this area.

Dr. J. W. F. Scrimgeour, courtesy Signalling Record Society

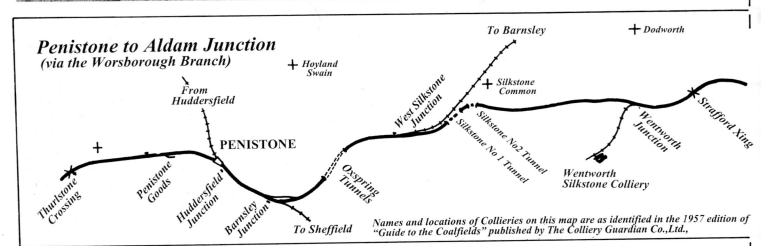

Penistone to Aldam Junction
(via the Worsborough Branch)

To Barnsley

Dodworth

Hoyland Swain

From Huddersfield

Silkstone Common

West Silkstone Junction

Strafford Xing

Wentworth Junction

PENISTONE

Silkstone No 2 Tunnel

Silkstone No 1 Tunnel

Thurlstone Crossing

Penistone Goods

Huddersfield Junction

Oxspring Tunnels

Wentworth Silkstone Colliery

Barnsley Junction

To Sheffield

Names and locations of Collieries on this map are as identified in the 1957 edition of "Guide to the Coalfields" published by The Colliery Guardian Co.,Ltd.,

(Right) Barnsley Junction, Penistone c.1890's: A group of permanent way men pose obligingly for the camera and a Parker Class 9A 0-6-2 tank engine, number unkown, simmers in the background in this quite charming period piece. Work has ceased for a tiny moment in time, though doubtless the foreman will see that all his hands are "hard at it" once the photographer has had his opportunity. The wagon behind the engine is marked "MS&L LOCO COAL ONLY", those to the left of the picture are lettered "Darfield Main", a colliery near Wombwell.

Collection of J. Suter

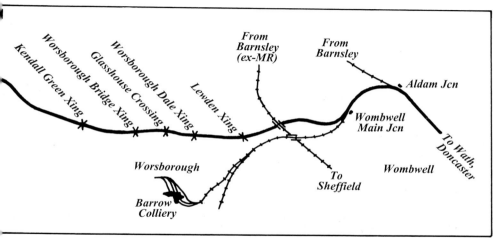

(Above) Barnsley Junction, October 5th 1950: 63223 comes slowly over the junction with a Down coal train. The Q4's (GCR Class 8A) were known to Gorton men as "Kitson Tinies" and are something of a neglected class when it comes to locomotive study. Perhaps it is forgotten that this engine was actually Robinson's first heavy freight design and anticipated the more illustrious 8K (04) of 1911 by nine years. The ram-shackle building in the background stands on the site of an earlier structure which is shown on the 1884 map as a "Tranship Stage". A further signalbox, shown as "B sig.box" is marked behind the stage on the 1884 map, but it is not known when this was removed. *Ken Boulter*

Barnsley Junction, October 5th 1950: Another Q4, this time No. **63225**, seen just moving over the junction with a further train load of coal bound for industrial Lancashire or Merseyside. A "crow" is sounded on the whistle and the fireman reaches forward onto the tender fall plate with his shovel to pack a few rounds into the firebox ready for the slog up to the summit of the line at Dunford. In the background a shunter looks ready to attend to a movement of some LMS cattle wagons being propelled through the yard here. Seen also is a cable drum from Henley Cables, doubtless in readiness for the beginning of work on the electrification scheme; the section up from Wath to Dunford becoming the first phase of this revolutionary project.

Ken Boulter

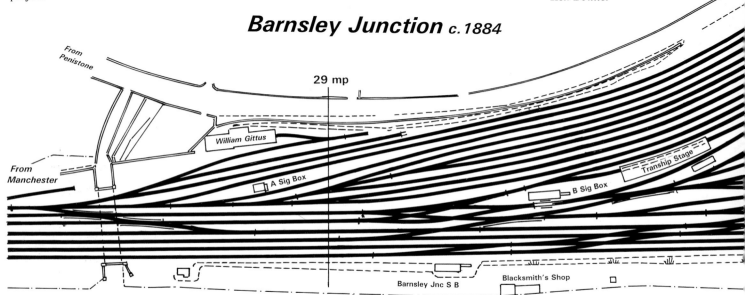

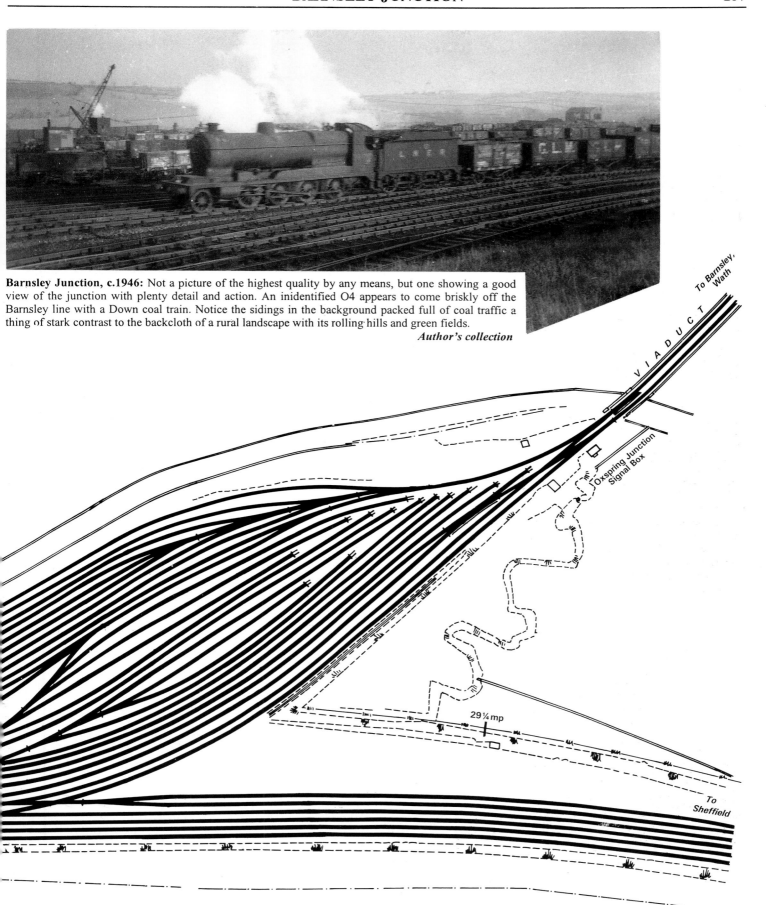

Barnsley Junction, c.1946: Not a picture of the highest quality by any means, but one showing a good view of the junction with plenty detail and action. An inidentified O4 appears to come briskly off the Barnsley line with a Down coal train. Notice the sidings in the background packed full of coal traffic a thing of stark contrast to the backcloth of a rural landscape with its rolling hills and green fields.

Author's collection

To Barnsley, Wath

VIADUCT

Oxspring Junction Signal Box

29¼ mp

To Sheffield

Oxspring Viaduct, September 13th 1948: Trains bound out of Wath Yard, having tackled the formidable 1-in-40 of the Wentworth incline, were faced with a further ascent, at 1-in-100, over the Barnsley line towards Barnsley Junction, Penistone where the line from Sheffield Victoria was joined. This passage took in two obstacles in the form of Oxspring Tunnel and Oxspring Viaduct where the railway crossed the B6462 road and the River Don in its passage down towards Thurgoland, Wortley and Stocksbridge. In this view, Silkstone West Junction has been left behind and a B5, No. **1680**, acts as a banker as yet another coal train is pushed up in the direction of Penistone. Immediately off the viaduct, trains encountered Oxspring Junction. Here were extensive sidings and two goods loops which ran down to Barnsley Junction. Entrance to these (Nos.1 & 2) was controlled by the two subsidiary arms on the bracket signal seen by the brake van. The two other arms are the Down Home signal for Oxspring Junction and the Distant for Barnsley Junction respectively.
J. D. Darby

The Worsborough Branch And Wath Yard

Reference to the map showing coalfields served by the LNER reveals a swathe of collieries runing north to south from around Leeds to a point just north of Nottingham. In particular, taking the Yorkshire town of Barnsley as a focal point and looking down towards Wath-on-Dearne, some idea of the vastness of the coal mining industry and its effect on railway traffic before the Second War can be gleaned. On a broader front and taking in what was once described as "The Great Coalfield", which lay in South Yorkshire, Nottinghamshire, Derbyshire and part of Lincolnshire, we are looking at an area which was estimated to hold some 49 billion tons of coal in the first years of the twentieth century. Within about ten miles of Wath itself, where the GCR had opened a sorting yard in 1907, existed forty six collieries. In the years leading up to the outbreak of the First War, the GCR were moving around 23 million tons of coal and coke per annum. Even by the advent of the Second War some 35 collieries in the immediate area were still producing coal.

The concentration of coal mines producing high quality fuel in the Worsborough Dale, south of Barnsley, meant rich pickings in coal traffic for both the Great Central and the Midland railways. The South Yorkshire Railway had opened a branch line to the Worsborough collieries from Elsecar Junction, near Wath, in 1850. A single-line affair at first, the route was doubled in 1876. A partial amalgamation with the MS&LR took place in 1864 before the company disappeared into the MS&L fold completely in 1874. Though much coal traffic found its way over to the East Coast ports, a heavy demand for high quality coal to feed the industries of Lancashire and Merseyside meant the movement of huge volumes of coal westward.

West-bound coal traffic from the Worsborough pits was, perforce, originally routed through Barnsley. Apart from a steeply-graded route, gradients of 1-in-50 and 1-in-76 existed, a level crossing at the curiously named Jumble Lane in Barnsley Town centre, confliction with local passenger services and the L&Y at Barnsley (Exchange) also added to the problems of coal movements.

The solution was to by-pass Barnsley by routing traffic along the Worsborough Branch and extending this from Moor End, west of Wentworth, to a junction with the Barnsley to Penistone line at West Silkstone Junction. The branch was made from single into double track in 1876 and an Act enabling the construction of a railway from Moor End Junction to the latter point was passed in that year. Though of only just over 2 miles in length the line took four years to build, largely on account of the need for two tunnels: Silkstone (or Worsborough No. 1) 74 yards long and Silkstone (or Worsborough No. 2) 289 yards long and interference from existing coal workings. The line opened for through traffic on August 2nd 1880. The total length of the Worsborough Branch was 7 miles, 3 furlongs, 6 chains. Not often touched upon is the number of colliery branches and adjacent sidings to be encountered, along with the various level crossings, along this most fascinating stretch of railway.

The topography of this route, from the area around Wath, through the Worsborough Dale and along to Wentworth and then Penistone, showed an almost continuous incline of varying severity; the *piece de resistance* being the section at 1-in-40 from Wentworth Junction through the two previously mentioned Silkstone Tunnels to West Silkstone Junction. Here the previous main line from Barnsley was gained and traffic continued along on an incline of 1-in-160 through the tunnel at Oxspring, past Oxspring Junction and then to join the Woodhead line at Barnsley Junction, Penistone.

Though, perhaps inevitably, the bulk of railway enthusiasm tends to centre on passenger trains and their working, it was coal traffic and from the Yorkshire coalfield in particular, that provided Woodhead with the bulk of its train workings. When electrification of the Woodhead route came under scrutiny by the government after the Second War, it was because of coal movement and the savings in coal consumption ensuing from electrification, that paved the way for the project to get under way again. Not for nothing was this given the title "Manchester, Sheffield and Wath" (MSW).

In our subsequent volume we will see much ceremony and flag-waving as passenger services got under way in June 1954. What must be remembered was that the section from Wath to Dunford got under way as an electric entity first. On the Worsborough Branch no less than four locomotives, two in front, two in the rear, were needed to bring a loaded "double" coal train (in excess of 40 wagons) from Wentworth Junction to West Silkstone. Thus was provided a spectacle without parallel on a British railway, four locomotives for one train!

When speaking of locomotive working over the Worsborough Branch mention must be made of the Gresley Garratt, a machine of 1925 vintage, which spent much of its working life here as a banker. The 2-8-8-2 monster, the most powerful steam locomotive to grace the British system, does not seem to have been a popular locomotive with the men from Barnsley, Mexborough and Wentworth who drove and fired it. This was on account of the massive 50½ sq.ft. of grate area together with the problem of blowing joints from the flexible steam pipes required to feed the articulated mammoth's two sets of cylinders.

Electric working from Wath to Dunford began in February 1952, cutting the time taken to move coal trains between the two places by over 50%. Thus was ended some seventy-four years of what must have been one of the most arduous steam locomotive workings in the country.

Oxspring Tunnel, c.1951: The eastern portals of the tunnel looking from West Silkstone Junction in the direction of Oxspring Viaduct. Unlike the tunnels at Woodhead and Thurgoland, on the main line, little remedial work was required at Oxspring when electrification came. The length of the tunnel is recorded at 559 yards.

David Ibbotson

West Silkstone Junction, July 1939: An N5 Tank, number unknown, approaches the junction with a Barnsley to Penistone local, Blacker Green Lane bridge is nearby. Below, at the top of the Wentowrth Incline, two 04's rest, having double-banked their train up from Wentworth Junction. Worthy of mention is the ex-GCR Refrigerator van marshalled in front of the brake van. At West Silkstone Junction, two engines will be removed and the train will carry on to Dunford Bridge with one engine in front and one to the rear. The chimney in the background belongs to the colliery at Silkstone Common.

Ken Boulter

Doncaster Station Yard, June 25th 1939: The monster is caught on camera away from its native heath. Seen awaiting entry to Doncaster Works for a General Repair, the 178-ton machine was away until August 5th. One must assume that it was not missed by the Yorkshire crews when such phrases as "The Garratt was 178 tons of nothing!" are on record.

G. Harrop/Author's collection

Approaching West Silkstone Junction, June 5th 1948: The peace and tranquility of this rural part of South Yorkshire is shattered as 04/6 No. **3906** and 01 No. **3901** blast their way up the last part of the 1-in-40 climb towards West Silkstone Junction. The photograph is taken from Blacker Green Lane bridge; the line from Barnsley curves in on the left-hand side. Notice the supports for the overhead catenary indicating the forthcoming electrification: of a type not used on the main line, they have an adjustable top bar to cope with the problems likely to be encountered in this area due to mining subsidence. The line over Wentworth bank has always been referred to by railwaymen as "The Plevna" and the name survives to this day. In the fullness of time it has emerged that construction of the line coincided with the siege of a town of the same name in connection with the Russo-Turkish war of 1877-78.

R. E. Gee

Leaving Silkstone, June 5th 1948: B1 No. **1167** pulls away from Silkstone station with the 6.08 p.m. Barnsley to Penistone train. 1167 was one of a batch of 50 locomotives built by Vulcan Foundry in 1947, having entered traffic on May 30th of that year. At the time the picture was taken, No. 1167 was allocated to Mexborough shed. *R. E. Gee*

Silkstone West Junction, July 1939: Once a proud traveller on the London Extension, D6 (GCR 11A) No. **5874** has seen better days as she heads a Penistone to Doncaster train near Silkstone West Junction. No. 5874 was one of the two last survivors of the former Pollitt 11A class, being withdrawn from service in December, 1947.   *Ken Boulter*

Barnsley To Penistone Line

Strictly speaking, only the section of the Barnsley to Penistone line south west of West Silkstone Junction should qualify for inclusion in a true "Woodhead" publication. However, these previously unseen pictures are included to add a little local flavour. The line from Penistone (Barnsley Junction) to Barnsley was opened in three stages before penetration into Barnsley town at Regent Street station was achieved in 1857. Silkstone station was on the first section, opened from Barnsley Junction to Dodworth, on July 1st 1854.

Silkstone Station, July 2nd 1953: Not quite a centenary picture, but near enough; C13 No. **67434** (a Barnsley-36D-engine) pays its usual call at Silkstone with a stopping train from Barnsley to Penistone. Silkstone station was closed on June 29th 1959. In latter days a new station in the area, Silkstone Common, was opened by the BRB on November 26th 1984.   *Ken Boulter*

Silkstone Station, July 2nd 1953: Not quite a centenary picture, but near enough; C13 No. **67434** (a Barnsley-36D-engine) pays its usual call at Silkstone with a stopping train from Barnsley to Penistone. Silkstone station was closed on June 29th 1959. In latter days a new station in the area, Silkstone Common, was opened by the BRB on November 26th 1984.   *Ken Boulter*

The Wentworth Incline

Two views at Moor End, on the approach to Silkstone No. 1 Tunnel, c.1951: (Above) An all-out effort is extracted from J39 No. **64833** at the head of a "single load" requiring a mere three engines-two are banking in the rear. Notice the varying sizes of coal wagons in use. In the background is Silkstone Common with houses built by the South Yorkshire Railway Company just visible through the pall of smoke. **(Below)** The same train a few minutes later. Peter Ward would have had plenty time to wind on his film and adjust his viewpoint before J11 No. **64334** and an unidentified Austerity 2-8-0, there were fifty at Mexborough in the last days of steam working over the branch, came into view. One imagines that, in a more health and safety conscious era, the guard in the brake van would have been issued with ear defenders! Some vans reportedly suffered bowed frames after repeated banking sessions in front of two locomotives-such was the colossal force required to move a heavy train up the incline. What conditions must have been like in the two Silkstone tunnels defy the imagination. *Peter Ward*

Moor End, approaching Silkstone No. 1 Tunnel c.1951: From a similar viewpoint, this time we observe a "double load" with the spectacle of quadruple motive power. **(Above)** Austerity 2-8-0 No. **90119** is the pilot engine and O4/3 No. **63716** is the train engine with a mighty load to watch and an ear-splitting noise to listen to. The tunnel mouth can be faintly made out in the distance. Despite the snow the two young train watchers (should we call them "Spotters"?) look to be enjoying themselves. **(Below)** Bringing up the rear are an O1 2-8-0 and another Austerity; neither number is known. Incidentally, the bankers were neither coupled together nor coupled to the train itself. Progress up the incline was, inevitably, very slow. When the train arrived at West Silkstone Junction (where the Barnsley line was joined) the two bankers were removed; the train then continued to Dunford, at the east end of the Woodhead Tunnel, with one engine at either end of the train in more normal banking fashion.

G. Newall/Ted Hancock collection

Between Moor End and Wentworth Junction, February, 1947: The grim winter of '47 with thick snow and ice must have made working up and down the bank an even more difficult job than normal. Here an unidentified 04 returns to Wentworth, almost certainly after banking duties. Sovereign Bridge is in the background.

Author's collection

Wentworth Incline, near Wentworth Junction, April 18th 1947: While considerable attention was paid by photographers to the *tour de force* exhibited by ascending motive power, trains had, nevertheless, to descend the bank also! 04/3 No. **3696** (one of the ex-ROD engines of 1917) clanks past the photographer doubtless at very low speed on the approach to Wentworth Junction. Coming down Wentworth, as a rule, the first ten wagons needed their brakes pinning down along with every other one after that. By way of a change, this is not a coal train: a medley of vans, a solitary tanker, a Weltrol wagon, sheeted and open wagons-something around thirty-eight vehicles in all are visible.

Author's collection

(Above) Wentworth Junction, n.d: Its giant bulk somewhat obscured by quantities of leaking steam, the Garratt waits at Wentworth Junction for its next turn of banking duties.

Gordon Coltas

Kendal Green Crossing box, May 24th 1981: Prior to bridging the site of what is today the M1 Motorway, the Worsborough branch crossed the road from Worsborough Bridge towards Stainborough, Round Green and Rockley. More traditional railway features in the form of "target" level crossing gates could be seen here. The single storey building held something in common with that at Lewden Crossing. A local enthusiast, or at least a more knowledgeable one, may notice that the "Kendall" part of the signal-box name is mis-spelt. The actual title should be "Kendal Green", the locality from which the name is taken

J. Bennett/courtesy GCRS

Worsborough Bridge Crossing box, May 24th 1981: At this point the Worsborough branch crossed the main A61 Barnsley to Sheffield road. Motorists in days gone by spent many frustrating times here waiting for the crossing gates to open whilst the ever slow-moving coal trains plodded by.

J. Bennett/courtesy GCRS

Lewden Crossing signalbox, May 24th 1981: Lewden Crossing box had an appearance reminiscent of a garden summer house. Here the railway crossed the road from Worsborough Dale to Dovecliffe on the GC's Sheffield to Barnsley line. Despite its diminutive size, the crossing box boasted a fully slated roof and a pair of full-size MS&L-pattern wooden finials. Cow parsley blooms by the lineside to add to the summer flavour, the hedgerows are out and Midsummer is but a few weeks away. But alas for the railway, these were the dying days of the Worsborough branch. The rasping bark of the steam locomotive is already a distant memory and soon the whirring and whining of the Class 76 Bo-Bo electrics will have faded as well. Soon, complete closure will be effected, with track lifting taking place by the end of 1981. *J. Bennett/courtesy GCRS*

Darfield Main signalbox: May 24th 1981: This box was actually at Wombwell and was situated about 200-300 yards on the Barnsley side of Wombwell Central station. Associated colliery sidings and a level crossing were controlled by Darfield Main box. The crossing was on a lane which took traffic down from the Barnsley to Wath and Rotherham road to Darfield Main colliery. Not all signalboxes on the Worsborough branch were to GCR design; this one is a Saxby & Farmer Type 5 box of BTF pattern (brick to floor with a timber superstructure). *J. Bennett/courtesy GCRS*

Elsecar Junction signalbox (n.d.) West-bound out of Wath Yard, trains joined the Worsborough branch at Elsecar Junction. Here diverged the lines serving Corton Wood and Elsecar Collieries. Though this picture is taken in the electric era, the signalbox, of all-timber construction, is virtually unchanged from GCR days. The small wooden building by the doorway housed a toilet, a luxury not found in all ex-GCR boxes by any means! To the rear can be seen compressed air reservoirs and the brick structure housing the track circuit relays and associated equipment. In latter days, lifting barriers controlled the level crossing where traffic on the Darfield to Wath road crossed the railway. *J. Bennett/courtesy GCRS*

Wath Yard

Wath Yard, Moor Road, east end, May 7th.1957: 02/3 No 63874 (a Doncaster engine) makes a good show on the Down Goods line as it pulls away with a west bound goods, probably a York or Hull to Mottram working. On the right, an 04 makes a simultaneous departure with a train for the east. The Moor Road overbridge can be made out between the two trains. Notice the fine GC pattern signal.

B.K.B.Green

Given the large number of collieries in the South Yorkshire coalfield at the turn of the century there was clearly a need for some kind of central point where wagons could be assembled and sorted in a rational fashion. Sir Sam Fay, the Great Central's dynamic General Manager, is thought to have spawned the idea of a such a yard following a visit he made to the USA. Fay's brainchild manifested itself as Wath Yard, a complex layout some 1¼ miles long. It was based on the "Hump" principle where wagons are pushed up a gradient and run under the power of gravity to a grid of sidings spread out in "ladder" fashion. At Wath there were two groups of 31 roads each-one for east and one for west-bound traffic. Each were fed from a group of Reception sidings, eight on the west, nine on the east side. A diagram of the yard was produced in the famous GCR publication "Per Rail" and shows the yard sitting south of the main line from Mexborough to Barnsley, just west of Wath station. Two "Humps" were provided: one controlled by "A" signalbox (for west bound wagons) and one by "B"

signalbox (for east-bound wagons).

The yard was opened in three stages: the whole of the east-bound sidings on September 19th 1907 and half of the west-bound on November 4th., the remainder of these were brought into use on Monday, November 25th. A Traffic Committee minute dated January 10th 1908 reported that: ""Considerable relief to traffic is being given by the opening of Wath Concentration Yard".

The whole project was very go-ahead for its time. Built at a cost of around £200,000, a staggering sum of money at that time, the yard points and signals were pneumatically operated; something the GCR had introduced on the west side of the Woodhead line under the direction of A. F. Bound-again following American practice. Motive power at Wath, too, was innovative with three cylinder hump shunting locomotives, the famous "Wath Daisy" 0-8-4 tanks designed by J. G. Robinson and appearing in late 1907 and early 1908.

Wath Yard, n.d: No 69904 (the first of the two 1932 LNER S1 engines) and 04 No 63704 and their train are on the Up loop at Moor Road signalbox at the east end of the complex. The locomotives will draw their train eastwards before propelling it into the "A" Hump reception sidings. In wintertime an additional engine was provided at this end of the yard to assist heavy trains.

H.C.Casserley

Wath Yard, n.d: One of the four 3-cylinder 0-8-4 tanks designed by Robinson especially for hump shunting duties at Wath. Nicknamed "Wath Daisies", Beyer, Peacock built all four locomotives: two appearing in 1907 and two more the following year. Designated 8H by the GCR, the class became LNER S1 and was replicated in 1932 when Gresley introduced two further examples. These differed from the GC's machines in being both superheated and booster'fitted from new; although the latter fittings were removed in 1943. In this photograph No. **69902** (GCR No. 1172) has pushed a brake van over the "B" hump on the top of the yard; this fed into the east-bound traffic sidings. The banking engines always worked bunker-first on the "B" hump and smokebox-first on the "A" hump. Around 1949 the S1's were tried as bankers from Wath to Dunford. Sammy Hancock, then a signalman at Hazlehead, recalled this event, something that turned out to be short-lived as water capacity was, reportedly, something of a problem. *H. C. Casserley*

Wath Road Jnc, Swinton, c. 1960: A view taken from a passenger train at Wath Road Junction (ex-LMS/ Midland Railway). The lower part of the scene shows Mexborough West Junction, on the former GCR. The line out of the tunnel is the former Swinton & Knottingley Joint line to York (latterly Midland & North Eastern Joint) over which the MSL/GCR had running powers as far as York. *David Ibbotson*

Wath Yard, Moor Road Bridge signalbox, May 24th 1981: Moor Road Bridge box was sited at the east end of Wath Yard and worked to Wath Station box some 200 yards to the east. Moor Road Bridge is of typical GCR design with wooden superstructure and a brick base and would have been contemporary with the opening of the yard. Notice the compressed air reservoir on the right-hand side to provide power for the various pneumatically-operated points and signals.
J. Bennett/courtesy GCRS

Willey Bridge Junction

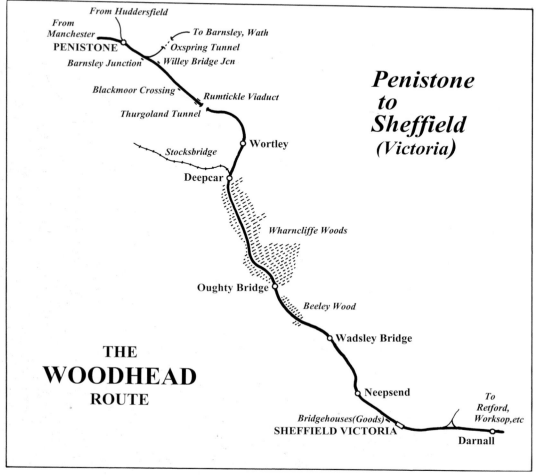

From Huddersfield

From Manchester
PENISTONE

To Barnsley, Wath

Oxspring Tunnel

Barnsley Junction *Willey Bridge Jcn*

Blackmoor Crossing *Rumtickle Viaduct*

Thurgoland Tunnel

Stocksbridge **Wortley**

Deepcar

Wharncliffe Woods

Oughty Bridge

Beeley Wood

THE
WOODHEAD
ROUTE

Wadsley Bridge

Neepsend

To Retford, Worksop, etc

Bridgehouses(Goods)
SHEFFIELD VICTORIA

Darnall

Penistone
to
Sheffield
(Victoria)

Willey Bridge Junction, August 20th 1953: Some 34 chains east of Barnsley Junction the four goods lines on the north-east side of the railway, which fed out from Barnsley Junction and its associated yard, rejoined the main line en route to Sheffield. As with the boxes at both Huddersfield and Barnsley junctions, that at Willey Bridge was an elevated, timber, structure to enable sighting of trains over the road from Penistone to Silkstone and Dodworth. Under the wire on a summer day in 1953, 04/8 No. **63613** clears the junction with a goods train for Sheffield; the junction Starter and Distant for Blackmoor Crossing, the next block post along the line, signalling the way. The gradient at Willey Bridge was a falling one: from 1-in-160 at Barnsley Junction through to 1-in-131. An MS&L map of 1888 shows a rock cutting here covered with spoil and labels the running lines as Fast and Slow respectively. The signalbox and overbridge features mentioned previously are clearly discernible in the background.   *K. H. Boulter*

Blackmoor Crossing

Blackmoor Crossing, just under a mile along the line from Barnsley Junction and Willey Bridge, overlooked refuge sidings which were positioned alongside both running lines. That on the Up side held 45 wagons, that on the Down 38 wagons. The box here was one of the few surviving MS&L-pattern left on the Woodhead line. Block working on the Penistone to Sheffield section did not come into force until 1878 and interlocking was unknown in company use until some five years earlier. Thus, the appearance of signal boxes, as such, would have been unlikely until those dates.

Blackmoor Crossing, early 1950's: B1 No. **61317** passes the crossing at the head of a 7-coach Up express. The train consists of a medley of stock typical of workings in this period: a Gresley brake third, an LMS "Porthole" vehicle, a GC "Barnum", GC Clerestory, another Gresley brake third and two flush-sided, possibly former LMS, vehicles. Compared to the later view, the crossing box looks quite smart-cream painting and the single ball and spike finial, referred to elsewhere, being prominent. Notice the trap points at the exit from the lay-by siding and the use of a ground disk, as opposed to a semaphore, to control the outward movement of traffic.
Kenneth Field

Blackmoor Crossing Looking very much a derelict and neglected structure, this was the box in its very last years. A close comparison with its MS&L counterpart at Silkstone station is interesting. *J.Bennett/courtesy GCRS*

Rumtickle Viaduct, late 1920s: A lovely sylvan scene, one that might well inspire those railway modellers amongst us. This is Rumtickle viaduct, bridge No 94, just over a quarter of a mile west of Thurgoland Tunnel, where the railway crosses the River Don. A fine four-arched stone viaduct, Rumtickle must qualify for the Woodhead line's most oddly named, obscure and neglected structure. The picture portrays pure vintage touches: a C13 tank, No **6058**, alas painted black, but still carrying its Robinson chimney, heads a Sheffield to Penistone local across the viaduct. No less than eight 6-wheeled carriages make up the train-copious passenger accommodation indeed. In modern terms, one wonders what the percentage occupation was for much of the journey!
Author's collection

Thurgoland Tunnel c.1932: Some three miles east of Penistone was the 14-chain tunnel at Thurgoland, sometimes referred to as "Huthwaite". Along with Oxspring, Thurgoland is perhaps one of the line's "forgotten" tunnels", such is the publicity and emphasis given to Woodhead and the use of the name as a byword for the line as a whole. In the wooded surroundings of the west portal of Thurgoland a Pom-Pom (J11) propels the District Engineer's Inspection Saloon out of the tunnel and up the 1-in-131 gradient towards Blackmoor Crossing and Willey Bridge Junction. Thurgoland tunnel was the subject of some interesting rebuilding in the post-war electrification scheme. (Q.V.) *David Ibbotson*

Thurgoland

(a) Branch promoted in autumn of 1846 (30/9)
(b) 2 mile colliery branch from Thurgoland to Stainborough.
(c) Powers obtained on 9/07/47. Built by Miller and Blackie opened on 22/11/47.
(d) Original intention was to carry it on to Chapeltown, but this never materialised.
(e) Tunnel referred to sometimes as Huthwaite Tunnel.
(f) Station opened on December 5th.1845 along with adjacent coal sidings laid down in 1845 also.
(g) Station closed as and from Nov 1st 1847 (also Oxspring)
(h) Branch joined the main line in a trailing direction towards M/cr. ¾ mile long-closed in April 1875.

Wortley

Wortley station, four miles east of Penistone, was opened for traffic on July 14th 1845. At the same time, in fact, as neighbouring Deepcar, Oughty Bridge and Wadsley Bridge. An early map of the railway shows a station with staggered platforms and four sidings situated on the Up side of the line. Two signalboxes, Wortley East and Wortley West controlled the proceedings; the latter enabled access to a trailing branch (from the Up direction and on the west side of the station) serving Bromley Colliery along with an adjacent lay-by siding and crossover. In latter days, the two signalboxes were replaced by one-plain "Wortley" standing on the east side of the station and sited 1532 yards from the box at Thurgoland Siding. A goods shed was situated at the east end of the Up platform and behind this was a small stone wharf.

Wortley in Great Central days, n.d: Seven of the station staff bask in the sunshine to have their pictures taken. By the looks of things, at least one train is due-Wortley's Home signals are pegged "off" and soon the platforms will buzz with activity. A joint Great Central & Great Eastern Railway poster on the Up platform advertises "Corridor Luncheon Car Expresses." Cleethorpes, an East Coast resort where the GCR had expended a considerable amount of capital, is proclaimed, too, on the hoardings. *Collection of David Green*

Wortley Station, Summer of 1939: Possibly one of the last pictures taken here before the darkening clouds brought forth the storm of war. An O4, number not known, drifts through the platforms with a train of single bolster wagons and presents a change from the otherwise almost relentless passage of coal traffic. Notice the staggered nature of the platforms, witnessed by the early map, and the quite charming appearance presented by the glass canopy to the station's exterior.

Ken Boulter

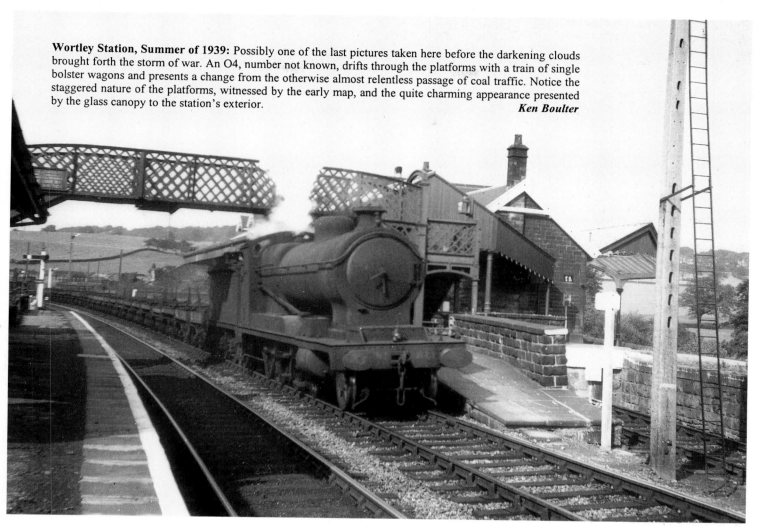

Wortley Station, August 8th 1949: The war is over and we have moved into the era of British Railways. Wortley still has its oil lamps and the attractive glass canopy is still there, protecting passengers arriving and departing from the Up side of the station. C13 No. **67411** is paying its usual call at the head of a stopping passenger train, probably a Penistone to Sheffield local. Notice the ex-Great Central clerestory coach at the head of the train. This is an eight-compartment 50'-0" third, ten seats per compartment coach. To diagram 39, coded 5034 and numbering forty-five vehicles, they were built variously between 1903 and 1905 by the GCR (at Gorton), Lancaster Carriage & Wagon Company and Messrs. Ashburys.

Ken Boulter

Wortley Station, May 24th 1951: An elevated view of the Up platform taken from the footbridge as N5 No. **69334** rolls in with a Penistone to Sheffield train. Notice, again, the presence of former GCR rolling stock at the rear of the train in the shape, once more, of a 50' Clerestory non-corridor vehicle. Journey times of stopping trains from Penistone to Sheffield over the years are worth a look. Typical times are: 1877-33 minutes with fares (from Wortley to Sheffield) of 2/- return (2nd class) or 1/3d (Gov.). 1938-29 minutes and 1950-30 minutes.

Ken Boulter

Wortley, Summer 1933: Here is what might be described as the "Classic" Woodhead freight picture-an 04 2-8-0, No. **5378**, at the head of an Up loose coupled empty wagon train, much of it from coal working. The station at Wortley is left behind and No. 5378 clanks steadily past the camera, probably at between no more than 15-20 miles per hour, in the direction of Deepcar and Oughty Bridge. A splendid MS&L water column with attendant brazier stands between the Down Loop and Main lines.

E. R. Morten

Approaching Wortley, 1933: C13 No. **6065** approaches Wortley with a 5-coach stopping train, probably another Sheffield to Penistone local working. The lofty lattice-girder footbridge in the background provided a fine vantage point for observations here. *E. R. Morten*

Passing Wortley, 1933: B7 No. **5473** leaves Wortley station behind and proceeds along the 1-in-120 in the direction of Deepcar. The 5-coach train, carrying the number 236, indicating a special working, includes some interesting examples of rolling stock. *E. R. Morten*

East of Wortley, March 25th 1948 J11 No. **4387** approaches the lattic footbridge with a train load c approximately 30 empty coal wagon en route back to the South Yorkshir coalfield. The panorama presents fine view of the track formatio contrast that of the Down Loop wit the track nearest the camera which merely an elongated shunting nec from the goods yard; a double scisso crossover enabling movement both t and from the siding off to the right, th neck itself and the Up main line.

East of Wortley, 1939: The pastor surroundings here show to advanta in this fine summer view. C13 N **6063** pulls away from the station wit a 3-coach local, in all probabilit another Penistone to Sheffield work ing. Notice, again, the presence of ex GC 50ft Clerestory stock in the trai formation.   **both: Ken Boult**

Deepcar

Deepcar Station, c.1880: A superb Victorian period view of Deepcar station, one of the earliest station views taken on the Woodhead line. The buildings, tall, stone-built, stately and with an almost ecclesiastical air, are those dating from 1865 to replace the crude structures erected when the line was opened. In this photograph we are looking towards Sheffield from the Down platform. Behind the platform seat, to the right, is a wooden buffer stop erected at the end of the Stocksbridge branch. It was from this bay platform that passenger services over this short line connected with Deepcar. Aside from the sheer fascination manifest in the appearance of the passengers and railway staff, there is a great deal here to interest the enthusiast: the ornate seats, splendid cast iron gas lamps-seen all along the Woodhead line and remarked on elsewhere. MS&L track in this period comprised bullhead steel rail weighing 86lb. per yard and laid in 30 ft. lengths. It will be noticed that the ballast covers the sleepers-a characteristic seen on the lines of other companies in this period. In the case of the MS&L the ballast comprised two layers: a bottom ballast made up of stone pitching 9inches thick; this was topped by a layer of "engine ashes" 6 inches thick and packed 3 inches deep above the tops of the sleepers. It will be noted that the track is inside-keyed-Elm keys and Baltic redwood sleepers being used by the company. At this time, two signalboxes controlled traffic at Deepcar: Deepcar East, situated beyond the goods yard in the far distance. Here were sidings and the goods yard itself, also the loop that ran round the back of the goods shed to form the start of Samuel Fox's private railway. Deepcar West, just beyond the Manchester end of the Down platform controlled the operations to and from the Stocksbridge Railway, a long shunting neck, as well as the entry to and from a short loop alongside the Down line. The two boxes were replaced in 1905 by a single box a standard GCR affair-which stood at the Sheffield end of the Down platform.

Jas. Bamforth, Holmfirth (collection of John Ryan)

Deepcar

Deepcar, originally titled "Deep Car" and sometime referred to as "Deepcar for Stocksbridge"- though the station never carried that title-was opened for traffic on July 14th 1845. Described by Dow as having "two inadequate platforms (170 feet and 233 feet in length), crude wooden shed (housing the booking office and waiting room) and three short sidings." The station at Deepcar was rebuilt in 1865 at a cost of around £6,500.

Connecting with the MS&L at Deepcar was the private railway to the iron works at neighbouring Stocksbridge, "in the Township of Bradfield and in the Parish of Ecclesfield." So much for nineteenth century cartography: The iron works at Stocksbridge was founded by Samuel Fox, a local landowner, in 1842. It can thus be said to have roughly paralleled the construction and subsequent opening of the SAuL&M. Traffic between the works and Deepcar station was horse-drawn at first, but it soon became apparent that such transport was both slow and inadequate. Having opposed construction of the SAuL&M Railway over his land at Stocksbridge, Samuel Fox is said to have courted the MS&L for construction of his railway of just one mile, seven furlongs and one chain, but the company were not interested. So powers were obtained, under the Stocksbridge Railway Act of 1874, to build a private railway to Fox's works at Stocksbridge from Deepcar-just short of milepost 33¼ sited west of Deepcar station.

The Stocksbridge Railway opened for traffic on April 14th 1877. The engineer for the short length of railway was one F. Fowler, the brother of Sir John fowler the engineer of the Forth railway bridge. It is implied that the structures on the Stocksbridge line were considerably over-engineered, something to the advantage of the latter-day operators who, with careful maintenance of the wrought iron bridges and minimal stiffening of the viaduct where the railway passes over the River Don, have been able to sustain traffic without any major bridgeworks or replacements.

Until 1931 the Stocksbridge Railway carried passengers as well as freight, the trains ran into Deepcar station and terminated in a bay on the Down side of the station at the Sheffield end. Inevitably, such a minor passenger service was easily supplanted by local buses and the five coaches used were sold off. A branch from the line served Messrs. Gregory's brickworks and trailed off at Henholmes Bridge. A set of five exchange sidings were installed west of Deepcar station and served to interchange Fox's traffic with that of the national system.

Surprisingly, the section of the former Woodhead line from Sheffield and its environs to the Stocksbridge Steelworks still exists today-as a single track line on a de-electrified railway. The line is still in private hands and exists as the notionally independent Stocksbridge Railway Company which in turn is a wholly-owned subsidiary of Samuel Fox's successors-United Engineering Steels. For some years only trains carrying scrap steel ran to Stocksbridge, but things have improved of late with additional trains running on a Monday to Saturday basis on or around Midnight with the occasional Sunday working looming up as well. Class 56 Diesels now providing motive power over the former path of a host of freight locomotives-latterly, of course, the famous Class 76 Bo-Bo's.

Deepcar, 1939: D49 No. **336** *The Quorn* enters the station precincts with a Down stopping train. Pictures of D49's on the Woodhead line are very rare and so I thought that this specimen, in lined LNER green, would make a most welcome inclusion, though its technical quality is not of the highest order. *The Quorn* began life as "Buckinghamshire" but was renamed in May 1932. When this picture was taken No. 336 was allocated to Hull's Botanic Gardens shed; as the leading two coaches are ex-North Eastern Railway clerestories it is reasonable to assume this is a through working of some kind from Hull. The Great Central-pattern semaphores controlled the main line, the subsidiary line leading to the goods yard and the line which ran around the back of the yard which fed the formation down to the Stocksbridge Steel Works. *Ken Boulter*

Deepcar, June 3rd 1950: From a similar angle to the view of the D49 we move on some eleven years to the post-war scene and the era of the state-owned railway. One of the by now ubiquitous Thompson B1's, No. **61059** in lined black livery and then based at Ipswich, makes its entry at the head of a Sheffield to Manchester express. Judging by the allocation of the engine the train could well be the through Harwich Boat train to Liverpool Central via Manchester Central. With origins going back to Great Eastern days in the 1880's, these services were a very well established feature over this route. Titled (unofficially) "The North Country Continental" the train will have left Harwich at 8.00 a.m., calling at Ipswich at 8.41. Travelling via Bury St.Edmunds, Ely, March, Spalding (Town), Sleaford, Lincoln and Worksop, Sheffield will have been reached at 1.23. Running then non-stop to Manchester, the Boat Train will reverse in Manchester Central before running non-stop again to Liverpool where arrival was booked for 3.40. The locomotive worked right through from Ipswich to Manchester, a distance of 216 miles without a change of crew-a remarkable feat. But for not much longer.........on the lower stretches of the cutting the support posts for the 33kV feeder cable for the forthcoming electrification are in position. *Ken Boulter*

Deepcar, May 28th 1947: By way of an interlude between pictures of passenger trains we return to more usual Woodhead traffic-freight. Here is an O2 No. **3974** -heading along the Down line with a through freight, by the looks of things a mixture of coal and van traffic. Notice that the GCR signals have been supplanted by LNER standard upper quadrant arms, although the GC posts and distinctive scroll-pattern supporting brackets have been retained.

Ken Boulter

Deepcar station, June 3rd 1950: Looking west from the top of the goods yard towards the station, the signalbox and subsidiary lines which served the yard and the start of the Stocksbridge branch can be seen. On the Up line two J39's, No. **64779** and another, number unknown, amble through in the direction of Oughty Bridge and Sheffield.

Ken Boulter

Deepcar, June 1939: "Director" Class (D11) No. **5508** *Prince of Wales* at the east end of the station with a working that appears a trifle unusual. At first glance a Manchester to Sheffield train is suggested, but the loco carries a headcode indicating a parcels working and, by the looks of things, is notched back into reverse. The second vehicle of the train is a white roofed clerestory coach.   *Ken Boulter*

Deepcar, June 3rd 1950: J11 No. **64447** sets back along the Up main line with a train of sheeted open wagons-possibly material of some kind for Samuel Fox's steelworks at the end of the Stocksbridge branch.   *Ken Boulter*

Wharncliffe Wood
and the Ewden Valley Railway

Near to Wharncliffe Wood was the Ewden Village, formed in the years 1913-1914 when Sheffield Corporation were busily forming a dam to contain Ewden Beck and form the Broomhead Reservoir. The Ewden Valley waterworks was served by its own village of substantial huts, complete with a church a cafe and a shop. A railway, constructed to standard gauge served the works and the village. It left the Woodhead line on the Down side at Wharncliffe Wood signalbox in a facing direction for trains coming up the 1-in-120 from the Sheffield direction. Five Manning-Wardle 0-6-0 tank engines were owned by the Ewden Railway. In the early 1920's there was much to busy them: materials were carried from Wharncliffe Wood sidings, puddle clay and stone had also to be transported. Even passengers were carried over the line and in the Second War trains ran from Ewden village taking workers to Samuel Fox's steelworks at Stocksbridge. Fox is believed to have provided the locomotive and stock for these workings and to have obtained running powers to do so. Excursions over former GCR metals were run to Cleethorpes in the mid-1920's; a photograph exists of a C13 tank heading a rake of venerable ex-MS&L 6-wheelers and a trip from Ewden village to Southport is also on record. The Ewden Valley works were inaugurated in October 1929. Sheffield Corporation paid the LNER maintenance charges for siding and signalling operations until early on in 1935. After that, the Ewden railway was dismantled and scrapped.

Wharncliffe Wood, early 1950's: B1 No. **61132** passes Wharncliffe Wood box with a Down express. (What has happened to the lamp on the engine's left-hand side, one wonders?) A picture showing one of the Ewden excursions in the 1920's shows an MS&L box on this site, but sadly, research as to its demise and date of replacement have proved fruitless. *Peter Hughes*

Approaching Wharncliffe Wood, August 28th 1954: One of steam's last flings over Woodhead, in the shape of an 04 hauling a 9-coach express, is seen as No. 63574 comes down the bank from Deepcar and approaches Wharncliffe Wood with the SO 3.15 p.m. Manchester Central to Cleethorpes. It was just three weeks before electric traction took over the whole of the running of trains between Sheffield and Manchester. Hitherto, engines were being changed at Penistone, steam continuing from there to Sheffield. Whether someone in the hierarchy decided that a Robinson engine should have a final outing on a regular passenger working before the crucial day is not known. At any rate it is a nice thought. *Peter Hughes*

Continuing along the downgrade which had begun at Dunford Bridge, the Woodhead line ran now through scenery quite different from that encountered earlier in its trans-Pennine passage. Away from the vast tracts of moorland and hill slopes surrounding the summit of the railway, more sylvan surroundings were encountered as the railway, now clear of Deepcar and on a virtual north-south alignment, the surroundings of Wharncliffe Wood are traversed before passing through Oughty Bridge and then Beeley Wood. Beyond lies Wadsley Bridge and the beginnings of the urban conglomeration which formed the outskirts of the famed City of Sheffield.

Wharncliffe Wood, late 1920's: A slightly curious combination, a D9 4-4-0 No **6041** and a J11 0-6-0 No. **5983** pass the sidings at Wharncliffe Wood-just short of the signalbox. The sidings in the foreground led towards the interchange point between the former GCR and the Ewden Valley Railway. The combination of rolling stock is magnificent-notice the London Extension stock, the second and third vehicles. The remainder of the train, all with white roofs, cannot be discerned accurately and the headcode belies an empty coaching stock working. Was this, perhaps, a delivery of new or refurbished rolling stock to another part of the system perhaps?
R. K. Blencowe collection

Wharncliffe Wood, n.d: The photographer has gauged the passage of GN Atlantic No. **4420** to perfection allowing us to study the fine outline of this celebrated locomotive type at the precise moment of passing milepost 35-a fraction east of Wharncliffe Wood signalbox. No. **4420**, seen in immaculate lined green livery, is heading an Up express-notice the Barnum brake third with the white roof marshalled as the second vehicle. From early post-Grouping days the GN large-boilered Atlantics (Class C1) had worked over Woodhead. Four were transferred to Neepsend in July and August 1923, to be followed two years later, by another six. The engines, displaced from their former home territory by advancing numbers of Gresley Pacifics, were in something of a run-down state when they arrived at Neepsend and were, consequently, unpopular. Pressure was brought to bear, however, and the Atlantics were sent to Doncaster for heavy repairs. Thereafter, they became firm favourites. Duties of the ex-GNR 4-4-2's included working west as far as Liverpool and Manchester, east to York and south to Leicester. Indeed, one turn took them as far as Swindon which involved lodging away for the loco men. In the Summer season, the C1's worked specials to the East Coast seaside resorts of Bridlington, Cleethorpes and Skegness. Workings were also recorded as far south as London's Marylebone and King's Cross. No. 4420 was withdrawn in August, 1947 ending a career of some twenty-four years on the former GCR and seven years longer than that spent on its parent system. Truly, a locomotive numbering among the real "Greats" of the steam era.
Author's collection

Oughty Bridge

Oughty Bridge, looking east, n.d: Truly, a trip back in time and recalling the well-worn phrase "in the mists of antiquity". This is the earliest known photograph taken at Oughty Bridge. Some facts, gleaned from the picture, yield clues as to the approximate date: the deep-ballasted track (of a similar formation to that seen in the early view at Deepcar) points back to at least the 1880's. A tall signalbox of distinctive MS&LR early pattern, named Oughty Bridge East, stands at the far end of the platform. Block telegraph working, as reported in the Silkstone view, on the MS&LR did not begin until 1869 and signalboxes with interlocking began to appear around 1874. The locomotive is one of Charles Sacre's Class 18A 0-6-0's which were introduced by him from 1871. A single-framed design, unusual for Sacre, the engine has two dome casings; these, especially the rear one have the distinct hallmark of S. W. Johnson who was Sacre's Works Manager at Gorton from 1859 to 1874. The 18A, number unknown and one of seven engines, is in unrebuilt condition with the single "weatherboard" in lieu of a cab. Similar buildings to those on the right (on the Down platform) existed at Hadfield. The gas lamps have plain columns and are in distinct contrast to those introduced later by the MS&L and in use from at least the early 1890's which had a splendidly ornate base. My guess, looking at this picture with its twenty or so onlookers, is that we are gazing on a scene from around the late 1870's to, maybe, early 1880's. And who were these people? The shunter in his pillbox hat, the old man by the platform edge in his "Billycock" hat, the young, the middle-aged and all the rest. Alas, we will never know.

Jas. Bamforth, Holmfirth/collection of John Ryan

Oughty Bridge, n.d: A later view at Oughty Bridge; this time looking west towards Wharncliffe Wood and Deepcar and taken from the Up platform. Jas. Bamforth's classic view was taken across the line by the bottom of the wooden footbridge. The platform buildings, partly visible in his picture can be seen in full here. A notice board on the side of this building is headed "WHARNCLIFFE GRANGE" but it is not possible to decipher anything else from it. Notice the platform lamps are still of the earlier pattern; the track has been re-ballasted, but the chairs are still of the inside-keyed variety. Headings on the platform bill boards proclaim "MS&L RAILWAY" giving us a pre 1897 date; possibly taking us back into the late 1880's. Worthy of a note, also, is the fact that in 1891 the MS&L accepted the tender of A. Lockwood of Stalybridge for £1050 "for alterations at Oughty Bridge Station". Out of sight, behind the station buildings, on the Down side, was the Congress Steel Works which had its own private sidings. Another signalbox, Oughty Bridge West, controlled further sidings and the access to a timber wharf which was sited at milepost 36¼. The RCH station handbook of 1938 lists a timber siding here as "Oughty Bridge Timber Siding". Also shown at that time are the Silica Company's Low Yard and Top Yard and Dixon's Siding which may have belonged to the steel works. The Silica Company became later the Oughtibridge (sic) Silica & Firebrick Co. Ltd. (1956 RCH handbook.) No timber siding is recorded at that time. *Collection of J. H. Turner*

Oughty Bridge, October 14th 1945: The war in Europe has ended some two months earlier; B17's no longer sparkle, but the trains still run and the sun shines. No **2853** *Huddersfield Town*, this time one of the Darlington-built "Footballers" of 1936, is at the head of the Up Harwich Boat train. The workings to and from Harwich from Liverpool were referred to in the Deepcar section and the title "North Country Continental" was not restored until 1949. Notice the steelwork erected here for the electrification before the outbreak of war. *Ken Boulter*

Oughty Bridge, 1939: A classic LNER period picture with a sparkling clean apple green B17 at the head of a train of Teak coaches and forming an Up express. No. **2871** *Manchester City* was the penultimate member of the second batch of the "Footballer" series of B17's. These were built by Robert Stephenson & Co. from January to July 1937. The name "Manchester City" had been allocated originally to No. 2870 which was subsequently re-named "Tottenham Hotspur" before becoming "City of London" when streamlining was applied in September 1937. No. 2871 lost the name of the famous northern club who, my Father always reminded me, were very much the top Manchester team in those days. In 1945 after being rebuilt by Thompson as a B2, it was allocated to Royal Train duties and assumed the name of "Royal Sovereign". The "Manchester City" title had been bestowed upon the engine at a ceremony at Halifax station on June 11th 1937. The answer to the seemingly curious choice of location may lie in the fact that part of the old Manchester City Football Club grandstand from the Hyde Road ground-just near to the GCR main line in Ardwick incidentally-had been re-erected at Halifax Town's Shay stadium.

Ken Boulter

Oughty Bridge, early 1950's: J11 No. **64443** enters the station with a short Up through freight working. The sheeted wagons suggest refractory material, possibly moulding sand or silica sand, there being several refractory works in the Oughty Bridge area. Incidentally, the spelling of Oughty Bridge as such would seem to belong to solely to railway parlance. Natives of the district relate that "Oughtibridge" has long been the accepted spelling, although mail is occasionally received bearing the "railway" interpretation of the name. However, Oughty Bridge station closed as long ago as June 15th 1959 having born its name since its inception on July 14th 1845.

Ken Boulter

Oughty Bridge Signalbox, February 19th 1983: The Woodhead route has now ceased as a through rail artery in this rather folorn view of Oughty Bridge box. Dating from 1908 this structure replaced East and West signalboxes here as described. The signalbox is of all-timber construction and can be regarded as a typical GCR building of this period; though the hipped roof with its fretted bargeboards, the small windows with sliding sashes and four-paned lights in the locking room, were all features inherited from later MS&L practice.

J. Peden collection

...through Beeley Wood

Those people who tend to think of Sheffield only as part of the industrialised heartland of South Yorkshire, historically linked with the steel-making and coal mining industries, might well wonder at the rural beauty found on this section of the Woodhead line. Through Wharncliffe Wood and with Oughty Bridge station left behind, the railway runs for about a mile flanked by woodland on either side: Beeley Wood and Great Hollins Wood to the east and Middlewood on the west. Beyond, further west, is the district of Worrall-a one-time farming area still clinging to its past, but now becoming developed into a select residential development with pretty houses fashioned out of traditional stone.

North of Wadsley Bridge, approaching Beeley Wood, n.d: The rural fringes of the wood are prominent in this view of C13 No. **7406** seen at the head of Sheffield to Penistone local train. *Peter Hughes*

Fringes of Beeley Wood, n.d: Now into the BR era, 04/6 No. **63907** slogs up the 1-in-132 with a loaded coal train. Notice, in both pictures, the presence of the steelwork for the OHL equipment-an indication of the preparatory work done on this stretch prewar for the electrification, only to be abandoned in 1939. *Peter Hughes*

Beeley Wood, 1930's: With the sunlight glistening on her boiler top and polished smokebox door hinge straps prominent, here is a locomotive looking every inch the member of a top-flight express class. Then named after a top notch football club, B17 No. **2871** *Manchester City* barks her way through Beeley Wood with a Down express-almost certainly from Marylebone. *Roger Carpenter colln.*

Beeley Wood, north end-near to Oughty Bridge 1930's: Former GNR Class J3 No. **4131** is making a steady effort through the sylvan scenery of Beeley Wood with a Colwick to Deansgate goods train. This engine was the only J3 to be fitted with both the vacuum and Westinghouse brake; the pump for the latter being sited on the right-hand side of the boiler-thus not visible in this view. Thus equipped, No. **4131** was stationed at Doncaster and was used in the Carr Works for testing the East Coast Joint carriage Stock. After the changeover to vacuum braking the engine was surplus to requirements and was transferred to Neepsend shed. The two brake hoses on the front buffer beam give away the locomotive's dual system. Though, inevitably, we are drawn towards GCR engine types in these books, a final mention must be made of this long-lived and well-established class of goods engine. The J3 and J4 classes had their origins in the 1860's and 1870's becoming known as the GNR "Standard Goods". No. **4131** was built by Dübs in 1899 and lasted until 1950, one of the last survivors of a most fascinating class of locomotives. *Peter Hughes*

Beeley Wood, September 7th 1935: The first B17's had arrived at Gorton in June 1931 and worked through to Ipswich on the "North Country Continental". Reports indicate that a member of the class was first used on a Marylebone train around June 1933. Thereafter, a mixture of B17's and "Directors" was used on the London expresses. Thus, "Director" (Class D11) No. **5511** *Marne* makes a splendid sight as she comes through Beeley Wood with a 9-coach Marylebone to Manchester express. Gorton men, it seems, did not take kindly to the new 4-6-0's and one, Driver Rickards booked off and went home, rather than forsake his beloved "Director". A typical journey time from London to Manchester (in 1938) was 4 hours 49 minutes. Before too many comparisons with today's times are made, it must be remembered that the journeys over the former GCR included around nine stops and the route mileage was 206 (to Manchester London Road). *A. G. Ellis*

Beeley Wood, northern fringe, 1930's: A further look at a "Director" at work on a Marylebone to Manchester train. This time No. **5503** *Somme* is working hard up the 1-in-132 gradient towards Oughty Bridge with a 9-coach express. A lot of derogatory remarks have been made about J. G. Robinson's engines in the past, but there can be little wrong with a locomotive that is putting in as much effort as this with a substantial train on a rising gradient and still has steam to spare–witness the "feather" at the safety valves.

Collection of Roger Carpenter

Limestone Hall Lane, c.1905: Pictures of Great Northern Railway expresses running over Woodhead are as rare as the proverbial hen's teeth. It is, therefore, with much pleasure that I am able to include this view showing a Great Northern 4-4-0 of class D2 at the head of a 6-coach Manchester Central to London King's Cross express. The train is passing Limestone Hall Lane signal box, just short of milepost 38. Here, the railway crossed Limestone Cottage Lane on bridge number 113. In later years, the well known Batchelors company (of mushy peas fame) would open their canning factory here on land just to the left of this view and behind Underhill Lane. The GNR began running a through service from Manchester Central to King's Cross on March 15th 1899, the day the GCR's London Extension opened. These workings were pure GNR, as distinct from the joint services with the MS&L mentioned earlier on. The Great Central had been able to keep GN opposition to its southern route to the Capital at bay by granting the company running powers to Manchester and south to Nottingham. The D2 class appeared in 1896. It was H.A.Ivatt's first design and also the first 4-4-0 to appear on the GNR. Though the number of the engine here is unknown, it is on record that six D2s, Nos.1341-6, were transferred to Trafford Park to work GN Manchester–London services, including, perhaps surprisingly, fitted goods trains. In July 1928, the Railway News recorded that Limestone Hall Lane box had been closed and that associated points (controlling the sidings at the Batchelors' canning factory on the Up side of the line and those to the electrode works on the Down side) would in future be electrically worked from Wadsley Bridge box, just under half a mile away, on the Sheffield side. Note that this is another exposure made with the celebrated Kodak No.2 box camera. One wonders what happened to the remaining 56 pictures!   *Authors collection*

Wadsley Bridge

Until 1888, when the station at Neepsend opened, Wadsley Bridge, standing at milepost 38½, was the last station to be encountered before Sheffield Victoria was reached. Wadsley Bridge station dated from the opening of the line in 1845. Improvements were carried out in 1874 which included the pro-vision of sidings. As at neighbouring Oughty Bridge, alterations were made here in 1891; the MS&L accepting a tender from Robert Neil & Sons for £2640 for the work. The 1884 line plan shows the earlier sidings as extending well to the west of the station to a point just past milepost 38. A Down Goods loop had been installed here by that time. Prominent on this early plan is the Steel Works of Moss and Gamble, actually "Joshua Moss and Gamble Bros." to give them their full title. Messrs. Batchelors (Peas) also had siding provision at Wadsley Bridge; both Moss and Gamble and the well-known tinned pea processors were here until the BR era. Cox and Danks, of scrap metal fame whose booty included not only locomotives, but also part of the German naval fleet, were also established here. But it was for neither steel, or indeed scrap metal or even peas that Wadsley Bridge was really famous. Generations of football lovers knew it as the disembarking point for the Hillsborough ground of Sheffield Wednesday, a cricket team once upon a time, incidentally! In this capacity the station continued for many years after official closure on June 15th 1959; indeed, a platform face was still intact at Wadsley Bridge in the summer of 1996.

(Centre) Wadsley Bridge c. 1906: Heyday of the GCR: GC Atlantic, No. **260** of 1906, pulls hard along the 1-in-132 rising gradient towards Oughty Bridge and Deepcar with a Down express. Moss and Gamble's Steel Works is clearly visible; the train is just clearing the station here. The coaching stock is painted in the choc-olate and cream passenger stock livery adopted by the company from around the end of 1903 as a substitute for the previous French grey upper panels with chocolate beneath. Such two-tone colours, a la GWR, were not to last long, however. A GCR Board minute dated November 6th 1908 recorded: "TEAK to be accepted as the future standard colour of the Company's coaching stock". *Authors collection*

(Lower) Wadsley Bridge, c. 1905: A delightful cameo; GCR chocolate and cream passenger stock hauled by a fully lined-out L&Y 0-6-0 passes Moss amd Gamble's works forming a Down express. A splendid array of GCR signals, notice the ring denoting a Goods line, all watched over by a horse, who hasn't the slightest regard for the proceedings and merely keeps on noshing away at his feed bag! The locomotive is an Aspinall "A" Class 0-6-0 of which 490 were built between 1889 and 1918; half of these engines were paired with second-hand tenders from earlier Barton Wright 0-6-0's when the latter were rebuilt as saddle-tanks. The Express headcode is inter-esting, but does not explain fully the situation. Possibly, this could be a London Marylebone to Bradford train as a balance working to an L&Y coaching set. Under an agreement dated January 26th 1848, the L&Y had running powers over the GCR between Penistone, Sheffield and intermediate stations. The L&Y were not to convey Manchester and Sheffield traffic via this route or, indeed, any GC local traffic between Penistone and Shef-field except by consent. The company received 33⅓% for working expenses, amplified as "9d. per mile for Engine, mileage on stock, and ½d per mile for Guards, and 33⅓% on special trains of Show vans etc". Incidentally, the cir-cular format of this most interesting photograph is explained by its taking on a Kodak No. 2 box camera which produced 60 circular images on one film. All you 36 exposure chaps please take note! *Collection of J H Turner*

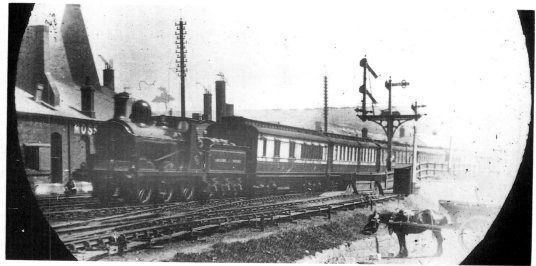

Wadsley Bridge, Septmber 19th 1953: Passing the site of the famous Batchelor's factory, C13 No. **67434** pulls away from the station with a Penistone to Sheffield train. Notice part of the famous Batchelor's monogram familiar to lovers of this one-time company's celebrated northern delicacy-mushy peas! ***B. R. Goodlad***

Wadsley Bridge, June 23rd 1966: The station in modern times, the obvious difference being the presence of the overhead electrification. Notable survivors are the MS&L gas lamp posts now carrying ugly, if more functional, "swan neck" tops and the nowadays much-prized BR "totem" station signs have replaced the wooden sign boards of the GCR and its predecessor. A GCR pattern all-timber signalbox has appeared on the platform, replacing the earlier MS&L box slightly further along the line. The track is light years away from its Victorian counterpart: continuously welded flat-bottom rail sits on concrete sleepers with a deep ballasted shoulder. Amazing to think that this, an (almost) thoroughly modern railway was to have such a short lifespan as a through route. ***Gordon Biddle***

Wadsley Bridge, 1930's: Former GCR Class 8G (LNE B9) 4-6-0 storms into the station with a Down express-an excursion working by the looks of the "570" headboard. The 6-coach train is a mixture of ECJS, GCR and Gresley stock fascinating combinations long vanquished from our modern railway. An overhead crane in the goods yard has engaged its lifting gear-probably for traffic to and from the adjacent steelworks of Moss and Gamble. The goods shed in the background appears on the 1884 line plan and may well have dated from 1874 when improvements were carried out here. A feature of the MS&L platform gas lamps is worth noting; unlike most other companies, these lamps were carried by an outer framing which supported the lamp housing inside. The MS&L did follow other companies in their use of the station name in the top of the lamp glass-clearly discernible here. Seemingly, when stations were closed and contracts let for demolition, a favourite practice was to smash the cast iron lamp post close to the ground with a sledge hammer. Thus the awkward and tedious process of digging out what was a deep supporting base was obviated! Alas for the charm and beauty of so much of our railway heritage, so needlessly discarded.

Author's collection

Wadsley Bridge, n.d: A scene looking east towards Neepsend and Sheffield. On February 27th 1891 the MS&L board recorded that they had accepted a tender from A. Lockwood of Stalybridge "for alterations at Wadsley Bridge Station". These may well have brought about the hipped-roof platform buildings with the deep awnings seen here. The signalbox is similar to other MS&L boxes we have seen-the box's position, at the end of the Up platform, is shown on the 1884 line plan. Notice, again, the deep ballasted track with the top cover of ashes and the inside keyed track - *qf* Deepcar. *Author's collection*

Wadsley Bridge, Late 1930's: From a similar angle to the picture of the B9 (previous page), the massive paunch of a Gresley K3 shows itself as No **2417** runs through the station with a morning express. An MS&L 6-wheeled brake van can be seen behind the tender. Perhaps surprisingly, such vehicles could still be seen, in identical positions, on expresses over Woodhead in the early 1950's. Notice the reference for the Sheffield Wednesday football ground beneath the station nameboard. No 2417 was one of a batch of ten K3's built by Armstrong Whitworth in the summer of 1936. When new the engine was allocated to Gorton, where it remained until September 1938 when it was transferred to Stratford. A steam heat connection was fitted between June and August 1938 when the locomotive was in shops at Doncaster. Thus, something of a reliable date can be gleaned for the photograph.

W. Grundy/courtesy Owen Russell

Wadsley Bridge, n.d: Far removed from main line freight duties O4/3 No **63888** performs humbler duties in the shape of the daily shunt at Wadsley Bridge. The trackwork is reminiscent of that from a Colonel Stephens railway!

Gordon Coltas

Wardsend Cemetery, 1930s: The section of line alongside Wardsend Cemetery and Neepsend Power Station seems to have been a popular spot with photographers over the years. Here, ex GC Atlantic No **5265** storms past Wardsend Cemetery with a Down express. The overbridge in the background, number 121, still stands and takes the public footpath from the area around Wardsend Cemetery and Club Mill Road over the railway towards Penrith Road and Longley Avenue in the Norwood district. *A.G.Ellis collection - courtesy of David Green*

........approaching Sheffield

After passing through Beeley Wood, then Wadsley Bridge, with its surroundings of steel manufacture, associated industries and connections to the nearby football ground, the environment through which the railway ran at the turn of the century was still one with scattered rural overtones. And though the centre of the city of Sheffield was now only a mere three miles or so away, concentrations of industrial might on the landscape at that time were nothing like as prevalent as those surrounding, say, the Great Central's approach to Manchester.

Clear of Wadsley Bridge, trains passed Wardsend Cemetery, the resting place of many of Sheffield's Victorian and Edwardian people and an area now sadly overgrown and perhaps best described as a beautiful wilderness. Although, at the time of writing, an action group has been formed to undertake some restoration to the area. Beyond Wardsend's peace and tranquility was the Old Park Woods Brick works, one of two such manufactories in the immediate area. Park Woods works lay on the west side of the railway, across the line to the east were the same-named woods. A contemporary Ordnance Survey map shows a quite extensive plantation with allotments, a recreation ground and a quarry on the eastern flank. This district also provided a name for the Old Park silver rolling mills-where a specially-produced sandwich of silver and copper provided the raw material for Sheffield silversmiths. Below Old Park Woods lay the estate of Park Woods Springs; a small housing development built up in the 1860s, doubtless with local railway employees in mind. Writing in Footplate Memories, Michael Smith, a one-time Neepsend driver, expresses bemusement at this name: there being no park, wood or, indeed, springs either !

At the foot of Park Wood Springs ran Wallace Road. Here were storage sidings for Neepsend engine shed and the scene of many photographs taken over the years of rows of engines out of steam-so congested were conditions at the adjacent shed. Right opposite the shed was Neepsend Gas Works built in 1852 by the Gas Consumers Company and in use until modern times. In 1902, the Old Park Woods Brick Works became the site of what was then Sheffield Corporation's Neepsend electricity generating station. So what had been a rural scene gradually became eroded and supplanted by industry. Running through it and serving it all was the railway.

Wardsend Cemetery, early 1930s: Looking north towards Wadsley Bridge, this view shows the end of the sidings from Neepsend power station. Bridge No 122 is overhead, bridge No 121 is in the background-notice the winding public footpath that led up towards Norwood. Clearly visible to the right of the footpath are gravestones in Wardsend Cemetery. The occupants, to quote from Thomas Gray, *"Each in his narrow cell forever laid"*, will not be disturbed by the sight and sound of Class B2 No **5424** *City of Lincoln*, rolling past with an Up express. The siding layout here was altered in later years, the two shunting necks becoming extended loops which fed back into the Down line. The signal in the background belongs to Park Wood signal box which controlled the proceedings here. *Collection of Roger Carpenter*

North of Neepsend Power Station, 1920s: A picture with almost pure GCR overtones on the Wardsend/Neepsend stretch of line and one that I was delighted to come across whilst collecting and researching material for this book. Class B4 "Immingham" (GCR 8F) 4-6-0 No **6099**, resplendent in lined LNER Apple green, is seen in a delightful summer landscape working hard along the Down line at the head of a five-coach express; two non-passenger vehicles are behind the tender. A small onlooker can be seen behind the balustrade of the bridge and other pictures taken here show youngsters observing trains-was this a "spotter's bridge" perhaps? *Author's collection*

North of Neepsend Power Station, Summer 1936: This is what the photographers came here for! Forget for a few moments the derogatory reports about the rough riding of the B17s and look at the splendid sight presented by a sparkling Apple green Gresley engine in full flight with an express train. No **2851** *Derby County* has cleared bridge No.122 and is making an all-out effort up the 1-in-132 towards Wadsley Bridge. Notice the train is made up, in part at least, of LNER Tourist Stock-the green and cream livery making a splendid match for the locomotive. Oh, for a colour transparency! Presenting a nice change from the more routine expresses, this is an excursion from Leicester to Blackpool, notice the "115" reporting number carried by the locomotive. The excursion would have followed the Woodhead line as far as Ashburys West Junction in Manchester, with the B17 taking the train up as far as Midland Junction. Here, a relief engine would have worked the train over ex-L&Y metals via Philips Park (the Ardwick Branch) and Miles Platting into Manchester Victoria for the final leg of the run to the Fylde Coast. *Cyril Spencer*

North of Neepsend Power Station, 1930's. Whether concrete footbridges can ever be described as "fine" depends very much on your aesthetic point of view. "Director" No **5509** *Prince Albert* storms under bridge 122 with a Down express. A crossing had existed at Wardsend in the nineteenth century. An MS&L minute dated 11 October 1889 records that; *"W Mc-Gregor tendered unsuccessfully for a footbridge at Wardsend Crossing, Sheffield' (£825). Let to A Haughton (£395)."* This concrete bridge, described in current parlance as a "bow-string bridge", and certainly not of nineteenth century design, connected Club Mill Road, alongside Neepsend Power Station, with roads in the Nor-wood district. It was demolished by BR in 1977; the public footpath that it carried was diverted over bridge 121.

Collection of Roger Carpenter

Neepsend Power Station, 1930s: A last look at this area before we head along the line to Neepsend shed. The slag heaps of Neepsend power station form an ugly backdrop to this view of "Director" No **5430** *Purdon Viccars* passing by with a seven-coach train, almost certainly an express from Marylebone. Park Wood signal box can be seen between the fourth and fifth coaches. The train is either stationary or moving very slowly; perhaps the photographer has used this to his advantage. Neepsend power station remained in use until the early 1970s. Today, the de-electrified single line to the steelworks at Stocksbridge runs through the landscape here; making for a lonely, solitary place with only the eerie, overgrown ruins of neighbouring Wardsend Cemetery for company.

Collection of Roger Carpenter

Neepsend Station, LNER days: Taken from the station footbridge, this view looks north towards Old Park Wood and Wadsley Bridge. In strong afternoon sunlight a J39 runs towards Sheffield Victoria. The inhabitants of the Neepsend district had to wait until 1888 for their station. An MS&L minute dated May 13th 1887 reported that: "Tenders for the new station at Neepsend included: S&W Pattinson £589.18.8d (Accepted). W.Mc Gregor £637.13.0d. C.Genney £736.2.11d." The station opened on July 1st 1888. The structure in the background is a cooling tower from the (then) Sheffield Corporation Neepsend electricity generating station. Built on the site of the Old Park Wood Brick Works, the station was gradually up-rated in capacity before being de-commissioned by the CEGB in the early 1970s.
Peter Hughes

Neepsend Station, c.1910; Here we are looking in the opposite direction-east towards Sheffield Victoria. The single-storey station buildings bear a strong resemblance to those built by the MS&L for the Macclesfield, Bollington & Marple Railway-a concern operated jointly with the North Staffordshire company. Of particular interest is the fine herringbone-patterned brickwork visible on the end walls of the buildings. Rising in the background are the terraced houses along Wallace Road, a familiar sight in pictures taken along this stretch of line. The lattice footbridge led from the end of Parkwood Road by Neepsend Gas Works, on the Down side of the railway, and connected with the end of Wallace Road and Pickering Road on the Up side. Neepsend station closed to passengers on October 28th 1940-doubtless a wartime economy measure. *Sheffield City Libraries*

Neepsend, July 8th 1934: Another chance to glimpse the lines of locomotives that rested by the house backs of Wallace Road. Looking at D9 No **5111** and comparing it with No 1027, we have a good opportunity to see how these graceful Robinson 4-4-0s had their details altered as the years passed. No.5111 has now been painted black; notice how, due to the disposition of the curved brass beading, the running number was awkwardly placed above the coupling rod splasher. Long-pattern ash ejector, snifting valve and "Flowerpot" chimney all mark the engine out visibly from "as built" condition. A C13, No 8063, standing in front and a B4 "Immingham" 4-6-0, just revealing its green-painted identity in the rear, complete the picture.
Brunel Univ. Transport Collection

(Centre) Neepsend, July 8th 1934: This view takes us away from the five engine storage roads and into the shed precincts alongside the water tank. D49/2 No **232** *The Badsworth* - one of the seemingly lesser photographed Gresley "Hunt" Class 4-4-0s - was stationed at York at this time. Workings from there, Hull and Gateshead would have brought D49s to Neepsend. In our context though, a D49 was something of a rare bird on the Sheffield to Manchester line. "The Railway Observer" reported, however, the appearance of No 234 *Yorkshire* on the 4.40 pm Sheffield to Manchester express on May 13th 1943; the same engine being used two days later on a local to Penistone. *The Badsworth* had subsequent spells at Gateshead, Neville Hill and Scarborough sheds. It was withdrawn from service in October 1960. *Brunel University Transport Collection*

Neepsend, n.d: A tiny fragment of Neepsend's existence-one of an almost relentless passage of trains both freight and passenger, engine movements, repairs and associated activity that went on, night and day, for well nigh on a century. O4/1 No **6246** storms past the storage roads in front of Wallace Road with a Down goods train. The sidings where the photographer stands belong to the Neepsend Gas Works. *Collection of W.A.Brown*

On Shed

Neepsend Shed, 1930s: A view at Neepsend showing the close proximity of the engine roads to the adjacent houses. Facing on to the railway are the backs of the terraced houses along Wallace Road, doubtless the domain of at least some of the men who worked at this shed. In strong sunlight C13 No **6056** awaits its next turn of duty-doubtless on a Sheffield to Penistone local. Peeping through the gap between the C13 and its neighbour, an N4 or an N5 tank perhaps, can be seen the outlines of a GNR tender, tantalisingly showing its lined Apple green livery and no doubt the property of one of Neepsend's celebrated GN Large Atlantics.   ***Author's collection***

(Centre) Neepsend Shed, n.d: A look at something different at Neepsend, by way of a change. This is a former Lancashire, Derbyshire & East Coast Railway 0-4-4 tank engine-class G3 No **6402**. A product of Kitson's of Leeds, this specimen dated from 1898 and became GCR property when the company absorbed the LD&EC on January 1st 1907. After the Grouping the class migrated to the Sheffield area, filling in on stopping passenger duties and working as station pilot at Victoria. No 6402 was withdrawn in November 1935, the last of the six members of the class to go.   ***Author's collection***

(Lower) Neepsend Shed, 1920s: Pictures of former GCR "Pom-Pom" 0-6-0s are bound to feature at least once or twice in any work dealing with the lines of the former Great Central Railway. This picture says so much about Neepsend, it just had to be included in this feature. The J11, with tender piled high, stands back-to-back with a compatriot 0-6-0 and faces an O4 2-8-0. Behind is a former MS&L 6-wheel carriage, the sidings being used also for the storage of coaching stock. There were five parallel siding roads here, sandwiched in between the Gas Works, the main line and Wallace Road. The five siding roads, some 300 yards long, joined the main line at the back of the shed building. This, in turn, housed six roads; the turntable and water tank being sited beyond these, as separately described. Showing well is the steeply-graded nature of the streets in this locality. Notice the copious quantities of washing pegged out to dry amid the house backs of Wallace Road. Pity the poor Sheffield housewives who struggled against the prevailing hostile conditions: an abundance of smoke and smuts-no automatic washing machines and miracle whiteners in those days!   ***Author's collection***

Neepsend Shed

Neepsend Shed, c. first decade 1900's: Parker Class 2 (LNER D7) No 709 stands on Neepsend's turntable with fifteen members of the cleaning gang posed around the engine. A bowler-hatted foreman, stern-looking as ever, eyes the photographer cautiously. This picture was salvaged from the effects of one Frederick McKone, a Darnall driver. Frederick, then a Neepsend cleaner, is seen in the photograph standing on the turntable at the rear coupled wheel. McKone had been through all the links, including the main line passenger with B7's, but finished, as was the case, apparently, on pilot duty. Looking at this scene should give us cause to reflect on the harsh, almost brutish, conditions endured by men such as Frederick McKone in the early stages of his career at a locomotive running shed. When this photograph was taken, the twelve hour day was still the norm, wages were low, conditions appalling and discipline fierce. It would be interesting to know, of the men pictured here, how many survived to become, like Frederick McKone, top-link drivers and how many more lived to draw their pensions? We often talk of "Glorious days of steam", are we really serious ?   *Collection of W A Brown*

Dating from the 1840s, Neepsend, or "Sheffield" as it seems to have been referred to, was the MS&L's main locomotive depot in that area for almost a century. Though invariably thought of as an engine shed, Neepsend was, for a brief period, also something of a locomotive works. The SAul&M relied on a variety of contractors for their locomotives: Kirtley of Warrington, Sharp Roberts (later Sharp Bros.) and Robert Stephenson & Co. being some of the better-known suppliers. Gorton, of course, produced their first engines in 1858, whilst Beyer, Peacock & Co., Gorton's close neighbours, rolled out their first locomotives for the MS&L in 1865.

Production of locomotives at Sheffield, under the auspices of one, Mr.Sharp, appears to have begun in May 1862 when No.83, the first of a series of five 2-2-2 engines, were rebuilt to the 2-4-0 configuration. How much actual construction was done there is difficult to ascertain; boilers, frames and cylinders, for instance, would almost certainly have been sent from Gorton. Given the numbers of engines rebuilt at Neepsend, some components must have been salvaged from earlier engines. An 1890 1/500 scale map of Neepsend reveals a quite substantial building sited between the front of the actual shed and the turntable. The shed offices, with a clock placed centrally, stood immediately in front of the shed.

In later years, another shed plan shows the most northerly shed road in use as a repair road with access via a traverser across the bottom end of the shed. These later shed plans do not show the previously-mentioned building; instead, a large water tank seems to have been built in its place-between the office and the turntable.

To what precise extent locomotive building or rebuilding at Neepsend took place we may never fully know. What we do know is that the place must have been an incredibly difficult location in which to manoeuvre. Little room for expansion was to be had at Neepsend; on its north-east flank, the shed was hemmed in by an adjacent brick works with a vast shale pit impinging on the buildings. On the south-west side, Neepsend Gas works-which dated from 1852-and a whole cluster of terraced housing, came right up to the railway's boundary. Away from the brick works, on the Up side of the line, more houses in the district of Parkwood Springs completed the shed's enclosure. ....*continued on page 230*

Neepsend Shed, early 1920s:
J.G.Robinson's first express design for the GCR was the handsome 11B (LNER D9) 4-4-0 locomotive introduced in October, 1901. The design was rebuilt in three stages of enlarged boiler and differing firebox lengths, from 11B, through 11C to the final development seen here, the 11D class No **1027** had appeared in March, 1902-a product of Sharp, Stewart & Co. She is seen here alongside the water tank at the south-east end of the shed. This is the structure referred to in the introduction, which appeared to have been built between the offices (seen off to the left) and the turntable and over the site of what may well have been the original repair shop. No 1027 appears in the final 11D form with 5'0" superheated boiler (fitted in July 1920, note the long smokebox), short firebox (four washout plugs) and piston valves. She survived into BR days as No 62312 and was withdrawn in April 1950.   *Author's collection*

continued from page 229 ....Neepsend's station, a latecomer which did not open until 1888, was situated on the western fringe of Parkwood Springs, a relatively open space compared to the tight confines of the engine shed.

Impending commencement of the Manchester to Sheffield line forced the LNER to look for another site for engine accommodation in Sheffield. This was to be at Darnall, east of Sheffield Victoria station where there was plenty of open space and a depot, big enough to house both steam and electric locomotives with their completely different and opposing demands of maintenance and repair, could be built.

"The Railway Observer" dated June 1943 made the following observation:-

"The LNER at Sheffield are now using the loco shed at Darnall instead of that at Neepsend. The change-over appears to have taken place about the middle of April. Neepsend shed is now deserted, nothing but piles of ash to be seen; the sidings where "deads" used to stand, however, still contains one engine-an L1 No 5338 recently transferred to Sheffield ex Mexorough."

(Neepsend's official closure date was April 10th.1943).

Engines Built At Neepsend Shed, Sheffield 1874-1880

Engine	Type		Date built	Remarks
400	0-4-2 Cl.11		April 1874	Accountants register says renewed 10/88
401	"		July 1875	
402	"		Dec.1875	
403	"		Nov.1875	
404	"	"	Aug.1876	Brass s/v cover & Salter valves; Smith.vac brake with twin ejectors fitted. Date of 1875 on numberplate. Scrapped 1889
80	2-4-0 Class A1		1876	5'-6" wheels. Cyls.16" x 20" (Reb.from Hawthorn 2-2-2).
81	"	"	1868	" " "
82	"	"	Jan. 1877	" " "
83	"	"	May 1862	" " " 6/01)
87	" Class 24		1867	" " "
90	"	"	1876	(Old No.64)
405	"	"	Jan. 1877	
406	"	"	June 1877	Details as for No.404.
71	2-4-0 Class 24		Feb.1877	W/drawn Sept.1902
409	"	"	Aug.1877	Ramsbottom f/box. Cab single s/window. Smith vac.brake with twin ejectors. Scr.3/04.
410	"	"	June 1878	Ramsbottom f/box. Smith vac.brake with twin ejectors.Fitted with weatherboard cab. Scr.2/05.
69	0-6-0 Class 6A		Sept.1880	Brass s/v cover & Salter valves. Smith vac.brake with twin ejectors. Weatherboard/Sacr(cab.Scr. 5/15.
26	"	"	May 1879	Cyls.17" x 26" 5' 3" coupled wheels. Scr. 11/13. Gorton drg.is endorsed: "This engine (No.26) built at Sheffield loco dept."
102	"	"	Sept. 1879	Scrapped July 1914.
71	2-4-0 Class A1		Feb.1877	Withdrawn 1902

The Gorton Accountant's register does not mention Sheffield in connection with these engines. This does not deny the possibility that they were extensively rebuilt at Neepsend, however.

Neepsend Shed; One of J.G. Robinson's "Sir Sam Fay" class, No **5428** *City of Liverpool,* standing on the shed turntable. This is the south-east corner of Neepsend shed; behind the locomotive can be seen the kiln and chimney of the Neepsend Brick works. City of Liverpool is seen in the LNER lined green passenger livery; cab sight screen, external lubrication pipe, long-pattern ash ejector and snifting valve behind the chimney all mark detail changes to the locomotive since Great Central days. A stiff south-easterly wind blows escaping steam from No 5428's safety valves to one side to reveal encroaching hillsides; truly a place where nature and industry rubbed shoulders. *W.Potter*

Neepsend Shed, 1936: The performance of the former GN large Atlantics was remarked upon earlier. Here is one of Neepsend's regular engines, No **4412,** standing outside the shed office in the company of one of her partners, number not known. 4412 was transferred here on April 27th 1925. She remained in northern territory until October 1946 when she was transferred back to home waters at King's Cross. *David Ibbotson*

Neepsend Shed, May 12th 1935: Former Great Central "Immingham" 4-6-0 No **6103** stands alongside the coaling stage at Neepsend. The stage was at the east (Sheffield) end of the shed, right alongside the main line. Despite lacking some of its Great Central appendages, No.6104 presents a fine sight in lined LNER Apple green-something denied to many former top-flight GCR locomotives at this time. *W.A.Camwell*

Neepsend Shed, May 12th 1935: A slightly wider-angle view of the Neepsend coaling stage. This time D9 No **5110** *King George V* is on show with the two crew members seemingly delighted that their engine is being photographed! Coaling facilities at Neepsend were primitive: coal was shovelled from wagons of 10 or 12 tons capacity into small steel skips. These were pushed onto an electrically-operated hoist and then via a chute into the tenders or bunkers of waiting locomotives. The electric hoisting gear and attendant chute can be clearly made out on the left-hand side of the shed building. *King George V* is seen with a superheated boiler which it acquired in 1923, a smaller (4'-9") saturated boiler having been re-fitted to the engine in 1918. This most fascinating of GC engines was withdrawn in March, 1942. *W.A.Camwell*

Remains of Neepsend Shed, July 1960: Though closed in 1943, the shed buildings at Neepsend survived into modern times with the site being used as a wagon repair shop. The full five roads were still extant in this view which looks north-west towards the former station and Park Wood. Corrugated steel sheeting fixed ad lib over the ends of the roof do little for the appearance, but highlight the parlous state of maintenance that such places had to suffer. An interesting visitor in the form of a Transfesa van stands on the second road. Of Spanish origin, these vehicles were frequent visitors to north-west England bringing supplies of oranges for processing into marmalade at Messrs.Robertson's factory in Droylsden, Manchester.

J.H.Turner

Site of Neepsend Tunnel, c.1938: Dropping down from Wadsley Bridge, past Wardsend Cemetery, through Neepsend station with its adjacent locomotive shed packed with engines, the railway was flanked by the curiously-named Macro Street on its Up side and Wilson Street on the Down. Now, just ahead, before Bridgehouses Goods was encountered, was once a short tunnel where the former GCR line burrowed under the houses alongside Pye Bank, and then beneath nearby Rock Street. This last thoroughfare led into Railway Street where access to Bridgehouses Goods was to be had-as we shall see. In this vintage view, an ex-GN Atlantic heads an Up express, comprised of former GCR and modern LNER stock, towards Sheffield Victoria. Neepsend, or Pye Bank, tunnel was situated where the brick cutting stands-just above the locomotive. Notice the rising aspect of the houses in the background above the train-hence the need for a one-time tunnel. There were three little Courts of houses above the railway by the bridge; these were accessed from Reginald Street. In the foreground, wagons packed with newly-chaired sleepers, stand on the sidings that ran along Wilson Street from its junction with Woodside Lane and Platt Street. Dotted around were the saw works, steel and file works, steel billet yard and yet another steel works. Not for nothing was this once known as "The City of Steel." Pye Bank Tunnel, sometimes referred to as "Neepsend" or "Bridgehouses" tunnel, was opened out in 1909 and Pitsmoor Road, which still stands today, took the name of the road crossing the railway. No sign of Pye Bank apears on the 1950s street maps, although-curiously enough, Pye Bank Road exists today behind Pitsmoor Road and off Rock Street.

David Ibbotson

Bridgehouses goods, n.d: A view looking from the footbridge mentioned in the adjacent pictures. The scene looks across the yard towards the Wicker, Spital Hill and Victoria Station. In the background, the main warehouse building lies alongside the main line, traffic on this stretch being controlled by Sheffield No 1 and No 2 signalboxes, the former seen on the far left-hand side. An abundance of horse-drawn carts and their attendant animals will be noted. The legend *"Pickford & Co., London & North Western Railway"* is clearly visible on two wagons-clear evidence of interchange of traffic between here and the LNWR's yard at Nunnery-about three-quarters of a mile away. But horse power for local movement of goods was to remain in use on the railway until the early 1950s. Above the railway, in the background, can be seen the houses on Railway Street, with Osborne Street and Denholme Street·running at right-angles. The sidings, packed full·of wagons and vans, curved away to connect with the main line at the west end of the Wicker Viaduct. *Collection of J.H.Turner*

Bridgehouses Goods Depot

Until September 15th 1851, when Victoria opened, the MS&L had been constrained to use the small station at Bridgehouses, a one-platform affair situated on the west side of the Wicker and Spital Hill. Thereafter, Bridgehouses became a goods depot, in which form it lasted until modern times. A striking parallel pertained in Manchester where the Liverpool and Manchester Railway, established initially at Liverpool Road, forsook this for a station named Victoria; the previous terminus becoming a goods depot which remained in active service until the 1960s.

Before Sheffield Victoria opened, the MS&L built a short connecting line, about ½ mile in length from Bridgehouses along to the Midland Railway's goods depot in the city-a place known then as "Wicker Goods". (The name was changed to "Sheffield Wicker" around 1852). This short stretch of railway, opened on January 1st 1847, contained a 1-in-25 gradient and ran through Spital Hill Tunnel, 300 yards in length. Over its lifetime, the line entered Sheffield railway folklore and became associated with "Fiery Jack." This name was bestowed by the populace in the Spital Hill area on a trip working from Grimesthorpe-on the Sheffield and Rotherham line-to the Wicker Goods yard and then on, via the notorious incline, to the Bridgehouses depot itself.

Loads, usually transfer workings, were limited to around 17-20 wagons and were frequently hauled by Johnson 0-6-0 tender engines. The traffic was collected from the Wicker yard and the train waited at tunnel Line Junction (with the Wicker Branch).

Here, the engine was dropped into full forward gear and the regulator was opened wide. Of course, the results were spectacular; sparks, smoke and noise being emitted in copious quantities-this was born the "Fiery Jack" legend.

One accident, sadly, marred the tunnel's life. On February 25th 1861 part of the tunnel roof collapsed, killing six men in the process. Land over the tunnel, which had been built using the "cut and cover" method, had been leased to Messrs.Hurst and Company who were engaged in building a warehouse and stables on the site. Warnings about working too near the tunnel's centre line had, seemingly, been ignored.

Its passenger facilities well established at Victoria, the MS&L took the opportunity to develop and enlarge the Bridgehouses complex in 1867. Spital Hill tunnel and the Wicker Branch were closed in 1940, but re-opened in 1941 to help traffic in the war effort. Final closure came in 1949.

One tunnel mouth survives to this day, a reminder of one of Sheffield's railway legends and a connection with the MS&L's first passenger terminus. Bridgehouses Goods closed in 1965, traffic being re-routed to and from Attercliffe depot. The pictures accompanying this article were all taken in July 1967 and the entire Bridgehouses site was demolished shortly afterwards. As is so often the case, the area seen in our photographs is today covered by a car park.

Bridgehouses, June 2nd 1948: Something of a rarity.B1 No **61163** pulls away hard from Victoria and passes Bridgehouses with a Down express. This was one of a series of preliminary workings that began the week commencing May 31st as a prelude to the famous 1948 locomotive exchange trials. The trains were loaded to 373 tons (including the Dynamometer car-seen here behind the tender). Departure from Marylebone was at 10.00 am, Sheffield was reached at 2.03 pm, departure was 7 minutes later. Arrival in Manchester was at 3.30 pm. On this occasion Gorton Driver Dick Ball was at the regulator, though No.61163 was a Neasden engine at the time.
Peter Hughes

(Right-centre) Bridgehouses Goods, July 13th 1967. Signs of ownership: Something old and something new. No record of the precise location of the "British Railways" sign exists. Probably it was sited along Chatham Street where road access was located; the stonework is, possibly, one of the supporting pillars of the previously mentioned footbridge. The MS&L cast iron tablet records the location of a valve for the station's hydraulic system-a form of power now long-forgotten, but well-established in the form of a mains system in all major cities where commercial lifting operations were performed before the widespread use of electricity. How many young men of the 1960s remember Guards cigarettes? At 4/3d for 20 such past pleasures seem ridiculously cheap today. No Government health warnings to worry us in those days! The torn poster on the gate pillar warns of impending closure of the depot and the transfer of operations to neighbouring Attercliffe.

(Below) Bridgehouses Goods, main offices: These offices were on the west side of the yard and faced onto Chatham Street; the half-demolished footbridge in the foreground linked the latter thoroughfare, crossing the main line in the process, with Railway Street. Though partially obliterated, the legend "GC RAILWAY" stands defiantly next to "BRITISH RAILWAYS."
both P.C.H.Robinson/courtesy J.H.Turner

Spital Hill Tunnel Mouth, c.1952: A less than perfect shot perhaps, although comparatively few pictures were taken in goods yards and stations compared to passenger locations-fewer still were taken at Bridgehouses! This is the tunnel mouth immediately east of Bridgehouses Goods that took the short line down under Spital Hill to the Midland's Wicker Goods. Despite the short length of just 300 yards, the steepness of the incline, at 1-in-25, is readily apparent.   *David Ibbotson*

Spital Hill Tunnel, entrance from Bridgehouses Goods, n.d: Looking towards Sheffield Victoria, this picture shows the disposition of Spital Hill Tunnel to the east end of Bridgehouses Goods yard. Builders' skips are in place and activity has long ceased here as the 18.02 Huddersfield to Sheffield Victoria passes by in the evening sunlight.   ***Collection of J.H.Turner***

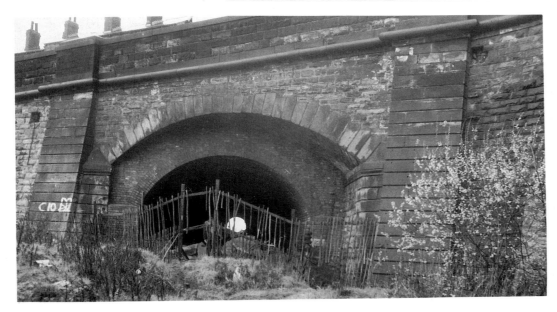

Spital Hill Tunnel Mouth, from Wicker Goods, 1973: After years of closure and attendant neglect the Victorian architecture of the tunnel mouth still stands; defiant and a monument to those visionaries who saw their railways as something of an institution.   *David Ibbotson*

(Above-left) Bridgehouses Goods, July 13th 1967: A close-up view of the side entrance to the main office building. Clear evidence of ownership is seen in the fine embellishment "MSLR" over the doorway. The purpose served by the cast iron arrangement of four rings is unclear. Notice the sandstone step, heavily worn down by the passage of thousands of pairs of feet over the many years of the office's existence. Gas piping is clearly visible, was Bridgehouses gas-lit to the end of its days, perhaps? Minor vandalism has seen off some panes of glass in the arch over the doorway; but perhaps the real vandals were the authorities who wilfully threw away this part of the nation's transport system.

(Above-right) Bridgehouses Goods, July 13th 1967: This is the complex of goods sheds that was situated on the south side of Bridgehouses Goods. Spital Fields and Nursery Street ran at the back here with the River Don meandering below. Abandoned sleepers and rail chairs litter the former siding roads, the curved nature of the layout being clearly discernible.

Bridgehouses Goods, July 13th 1967: Two views of the main goods shed which fronted onto the main line in and out of Sheffield Victoria.
(Centre-right) The main line is off to the left, notice the overhead catenary supports; the goods shed on the south side of the yard stands off to the right. Note the profile of the Royal Victoria Station Hotel to the left of the chimney stack.
(Lower-right) The opposite hand view of the shed with platform for road access clearly visible. Thieves, in the form of lead and tile strippers, have plundered the roofs of the adjacent office buildings. The small shunters' cabin, with its fretted bargeboards, is reminiscent of a GCR signalbox. New timber has been provided all along the end of the goods shed wall. Railwaymen have often cynically remarked that a renewal or a re-painting of a structure was a sure sign of an impending closure! Perhaps they were right.
P.C.H Robinson/courtesy of J.H.Turner

Sheffield Victoria

Sheffield Victoria, n.d: No train is in immediate sight which gives us a chance to spend a few moments gazing west in the direction of Bridgehouses and Neepsend. To the right is Sheffield No.3, a signalbox of typical Great Central design which was replaced at electrification by a more modern box further east. This earlier box can be seen in a later view taken from the Wicker. Sweeping off to the right are the Up loops installed in 1899 as part of a package of improvements to the station. Plenty of interest awaits the signalling enthusiast-a splendid 3-post bracket signal is pure GC, topped by three of those massive ball and spike finials. More GCR types abound further down the line, while LNER standard arms can be seen controlling traffic on the Up line. Within the cluster of buildings behind the signalbox in the right-hand background can be seen Joshua Wigfull's flour mill; behind this was the Wicker Iron Works, one of many such small concerns that existed at one time right in the heart of this city. Away on the left can be seen Bridgehouses Goods; a tank locomotive stands outside on shunting duties. *Courtesy GCRS*

Sheffield Victoria

As mentioned elsewhere, Victoria was the MS&L's second home in Sheffield and, though not a terminus as such, the station is, almost, the end of the line for this journey over the Woodhead Line at the present time. The station opened for passengers on September 15th 1851. Entering the city from the west, the railway was carried into the station over a 72ft. masonry viaduct some 40 feet above the thoroughfare known as "The Wicker." In consequence, the viaduct has always been known as "The Wicker Arches"-a magnificent structure indeed. The somewhat curiously-named thoroughfare is said to have taken its name from Wicker baskets that were woven by local women, having obtained their raw materials from Willows growing on the banks of the nearby River Don.

Mention of the Wicker brings to mind the original station of the Sheffield and Rotherham Railway which was built on Savile Street, a thoroughfare situated at the junction of the Wicker and Spital Hill. Opened on November 1st 1838, this station became known as "Sheffield Wicker" from around 1852 (Q.V. Bridgehouses Goods). The Sheffield and Rotherham Railway were taken over by the Midland in 1844. The company's Wicker station remained in passenger use until February 1870 when the Midland Railway's station opened on the present site.

John Fowler, perhaps better known for his achievement in Scotland with the Forth Bridge, was the engineer in charge of the overall planning of the Victoria station and the Wicker arches.

Fowler must have been a busy man in the late 1840s and early '50s. MS&L minutes report him at work with New Holland Pier (February 1848), Grimsby Docks (September 1849) and the Woodhead tunnels (1851 and 1853). Fowler remained as consulting engineer to the MS&L until 1873 when he was replaced by Charles Liddell, on October 3rd.

Sheffield Victoria was conceived as a single island platform, some 300 yards long and 40 ft. wide with bays inset at either end. A glass and iron roof, 400 feet long and of ridge and furrow pattern covered the station buildings These structures were on the south-west side of the complex and were reached via the station approach road: a 1-in-30 incline some 300 yards long and 30 feet wide. Contemporary literature described Victoria as: "this costly station covered with a light glass roof like that of the Crystal Palace." Flanking the station, at the top left-hand side of the approach, was the Royal Victoria Hotel opened, despite fierce local opposition apparently, on September 23rd 1862. The idea of a hotel adjacent to the station had been floated in 1856. A company-"The Sheffield Hotel Company"-was set up in 1859 with both the Great Northern and the MS&L themselves as subscribers. It will be remembered that the GNR had been joint operators of the King's Cross to Manchester expresses with the MS&L since 1857 and, thus, had a vested interest in things Sheffield. Parallel with the hotel development was the Great Northern's success in gaining a joint tenancy agreement for the use of Victoria station at

Wicker Arches, July 1st.1905: All the pomp and pageantry of Edwardian Britain is seen to full effect in this view of the arches, richly decorated for the visit to Sheffield of King Edward VII and Queen Alexandra. Onlookers gaze down from the top of the viaduct where MS&L 6-wheel, 5-compartment stock appears. By the looks of things the cluster of tramcars is stationary, so maybe the royal progress has passed, or is about to pass by. This illustration first appeared in the Great Central Railway Journal Volume 1 No.3-September 1905. *Collection of Ted Hancock*

a cost of £25,000.

As with large railway stations almost everywhere in the nineteenth century, Sheffield Victoria was enlarged and altered as traffic patterns changed and train workings developed. A new roof was provided in 1865 and the station was extended ten years later at a cost of £8,442.00-sanction for this was obtained in November 1873. City status was conferred on Sheffield in 1893 and, as in Manchester, small boroughs outside the immediate city boundary were gradually absorbed over the years ahead.

The 1890s saw the horizons of the MS&L widened in a southerly direction under Watkin's chairmanship. Strange how the dream of this Victorian entrepreneur: a direct rail link via a Channel tunnel from Manchester to Paris was still being hailed as something of a crackpot idea in even fairly recent railway literature. Now that old idea has become a reality; what a shame that Watkin's railway can no longer play any part in it. Principal amongst expansion south of Sheffield was, of course, the London Extension. But before considering this, there were other things of ultimate consequence for traffic to and from Victoria.

A minute dated January 10th 1890 records tenders in hand for construction of what were known as "The Derbyshire Lines." These are described in MS&L records as ..."*construction from Beighton to Chesterfield and branches.*" The railway would penetrate the Derbyshire and North Nottinghamshire coalfields via numerous colliery branches and would tie in with the Great Northern at Annesley. Eleven tenders were submitted to the company; notable amongst these was that of Logan and Hemingway who would be much involved with the London Extension and other works and J.D.Nowell, who built the Manchester Central Station Railway. After much fascinating deliberation with a concern known as Baldry and Yerbung, Logan and Hemingway built the Derbyshire Lines for some £225,000. Full opening of the lines was complete by July 1893. Incidentally, mention of Beighton in south Yorkshire, brings to mind an even earlier southern route to the Capital than via the through workings with the Great Northern mentioned in the Introduction. It was via Beighton Junction that passengers from Sheffield's Bridgehouses station could travel to London. Changing trains at Eckington, on the Midland main line, through trains to London (King's Cross) ran from 1856, though the service reportedly finished sometime after 1857.

Sheffield Victoria, c.mid-1920's: Taken from the lofty aspects of the Royal Victoria Hotel, here is Sheffield Victoria in early LNER days with a profusion of west-bound traffic to delight the onlooker. Out along the arched viaduct, over Walker Street and towards Bridgehouses, two locomotives-a "Director" and a tank engine are seen. The 4-4-0 blows off furiously, the "peg" has come off and the ensemble prepares to move forward. Further back towards the camera, a "Pom Pom" moves a van, still lettered "GC"; to one side; open wagons, one lettered "A I C" and two others bearing the "Shireoaks" legend make their appearance. The small building in the foreground housed a passenger lift which, as can be seen, provided the facility to descend to and from the Wicker upon payment of one penny-a facility which the thrifty citizens of Sheffield were apparently reluctant to avail themselves of! A staircase provided a somewhat laborious alternative. On the opposite side of the Wicker, on the corner of Walker Street, can be seen one of the city's less prestigious hotels-The Station Hotel. A backdrop is provided by the outlines of Joshua Wigfull's corn and flour mill; the chimney and grain elevator providing landmarks.

J.Peden collection

The Derbyshire Lines were really the springboard from which the thrust south to Marylebone would develop. Work began on the London Extension in October 1894. It is worth noting that the Sheffield steel makers benefited well from this new railway: the estimated 35,000 tons of rails needed were supplied by three different concerns: Steel, Peech & Tozer, Samuel Fox, whose concern we met at Deepcar and Charles Cammell from Penistone. As a consequence of the heavier traffic implicit from the new railway, Victoria was enlarged as part of a £100,000 package. In particular, the Wicker viaduct was widened to accommodate goods avoiding lines and a new Up loop was installed in 1899 as well. A new Down loop was added in 1906, a contract for £21,572.5.0d having been awarded to George Longden & Sons Ltd.of Neepsend on October 5th.

Motive power using Sheffield Victoria over the 120 or so years of its existence was as wide and varied as that at almost any other station. From early beginnings with 2-2-2 types, coke-burning locomotives obtained from Robert Stephenson & Co., the station would have seen the plethora of early SAuL&M engines, un-numbered and bearing names from Greek mythology. What a stroke of genius it was when, over a century later, some of these names appeared, albeit briefly, attached to electric locomotives. And how massive the time scale of all this development seems to us today. When the first trains ran through the Woodhead Tunnel it was a mere twenty-odd years since Faraday's discovery of electro-magnetic rotation. Yet, at the time of Victoria's untimely demise, electric railway traction had been seen as the way forward for railway propulsion, but was to be all but abandoned over the route that served it.

So through to the period from the mid-1860s to 1880s and beyond when Sacré locomotive types, most with double frames, would have been the order of the day. This was a period of rich green livery for locomotives, something that was to be perpetuated in GC and LNE days. What handsome beasts those Sacré Class 23 goods 0-6-0s must have been; with their flared smokebox wingplates and polished brass throatplate cleading to their fireboxes. Then, the whole gamut of Parker, Pollitt and Robinson locomotives would have sallied forth through the platforms. The Gresley era, which began, of course, on the Great Northern, eventually brought forth the sight of Pacifics here for the first time. Visitors came to Sheffield Victoria from other pre-Group companies: the fine-looking Great Eastern 4-6-0s, better known as B12s, North Eastern Railway 4-4-0s and Atlantics, Lancashire & Yorkshire Railway engines, in stately lined black, working to and from Huddersfield via Penistone.

The post-WWII era saw the end of many of the GC types that had long frequented this city of steel and cutlery. Some might think the Thompson B1s that followed to be, somehow, indifferent and inferior. Whatever your opinions are, this coverage of the Woodhead line ends in that part of the steam era. What follows should provide a good representation of the delights once found between and alongside Victoria's platforms. Beyond the steam era saw, eventually, a decline that, sadly, proved to be terminal. But stop. Put this to one side for a few moments and enjoy Victoria's former visitors.

Wicker Arches, c.1935: Here, the magnificent 72 feet span of the central arch shows, again, to advantage. In the foreground are two of the Sheffield Corporation tramcars built by Brush of Loughborough, No **393** in 1921 and No **51** in 1925, both lasting in service until 1954. Each tramcar is in immaculate condition, a hallmark of the Sheffield fleet. To the right is a Sheffield AEC double-deck bus, believed to be the only known shot of No 261-**BMG 969** with bodywork by Park Royal and an ex AEC demonstrator. Notice the LNER Morris Commercial delivery and collection van which is parked just in front of the passenger lift and the long flight of steps which gave access to the station and adjoining Royal Victoria Hotel. Both the lift shaft and steps survive to this day, although derelict and out of use. Behind the van is one of the famous Sillitoe Police Boxes. Once a common sight throughout the city, only one survives today. The boxes were named after the Sheffield Chief Constable, Captain Percy Sillitoe. Returning to the railway again, Sheffield No 3 signal box can be seen, again, on top of the arch. This, along with the attendant semaphores, survived until electrification in 1954.
Author's collection

Wicker Arches, c.1966: A summer afternoon in Sheffield. Two World wars have been fought since the days of Edwardian Britain and the visit of "King Teddy". From almost the same spot as our 1905 picture, here is contemporary Sheffield looking across the Wicker and up towards Spital Hill. Of our few views of the Wicker Arches, this one probably shows best the fine central arch with its gentle, graceful curve and the two side arches topped by the beautifully carved armorial devices from Victorian days. A foreigner, in the form of "Jubilee" No **45581** *Bihar and Orissa* waits at the Home signal on the viaduct for the road out towards Bridgehouses and Wadsley Bridge with a Poole to Bradford train. By today's standards, traffic is sparse-just a small knot of vehicles at the junction with Spital Hill where the Sheffield Corporation bus descends. To railway enthusiasts at any rate, the "Jubilee" presents something of a timeless sight. Yet, so many touches at street level date this photograph: the flashing "Belisha beacons" by the zebra crossing, the young Boy Scout in short trousers striding out purposefully, "NO ENTRY" appearing on the road sign; while the sight of an Austin Mini and its Clubman counterpart represent rare sights today.

Wicker Arches, April 1st 1996: Almost a century after its demise, the title MANCHESTER, SHEFFIELD & LINCOLNSHIRE RAILWAY COMPANY, superbly carved in the stonework, stands defiantly, though sharing its perch with a few errant ferns! Only the sight of the yellow box junction on the roadway below betrays the date of the photograph. What masters of style the Victorians were. *Author*

Arches west of Sheffield Victoria, c.1945/46: Having crossed The Wicker, the railway out of Sheffield continued on a viaduct as far as Bridgehouses. Here is "Director" No **5511** *Marne* carrying "express lights" and pulling hard out of the station, bound for Penistone and Manchester. In front of the photographer is Andrew Street, behind that is Walker Street. The two thoroughfares joined Johnson Street which backed on to part of Bridgehouses Goods. The houses on these two streets were demolished during the Second War, possibly as a result of bomb damage which was inflicted heavily both here and at Neepsend. Standing behind the railway are the Star Corn Mills of Messrs. Joshua Wigfull & Sons Ltd. Wigfull's title along with the names-"Diamond Star" and "Morning Star" patent flours stand out below the bricked-up arches, the lower part of which is in use as garaging for their lorries. One such, **CWB 421**, is seen pulling away. Laden with hessian sacks, each holding 140 lb.of flour, this is dead weight indeed! The corn mills dominate the skyline above the railway and were a familiar sight here for many years. Wigfulls were obviously proud of their STARBROWN flour-The Brown Bread you'll Like Better! *David Ibbotson*

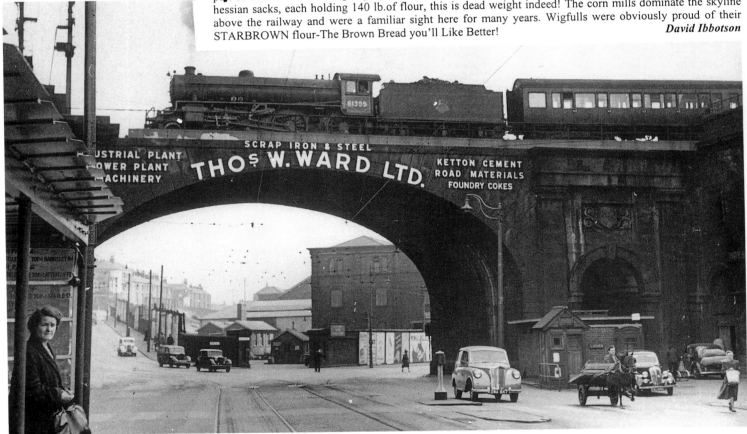

Wicker Arches, early 1950's: One of the hardest jobs when writing and editing books such as "Woodhead" is the decision-making process necessary to produce a balanced selection of pictures. Lots and lots of material had been accumulated for the Victoria selection and the final pruning was far from easy. I had no problem, however, when I looked at this picture-falling as it did firmly into the "must have" category. Howard Turner's splendid study sums up so much of the post-War railway era in this part of the world: B1 No **61399** strides firmly out over the Wicker arch, westbound with a stopping train. And what GC enthusiast would not want to travel in that splendid Matchboard corridor carriage-with an open window behind the tender of a B1 thrown in as a bonus! The colour light era has still to arrive, notice the GCR-finialled semaphore posts. Further delights ensue down below: this is still the era of the tramcar, Sheffield retaining her distinctive blue and cream-liveried vehicles until 1960. To the right of the arch can be seen the rear of the former Midland Railway's Wicker Goods depot on Savile Street, the "opposition" for the MS&L and their successors here at one time. Coming along the Wicker a pony and cart trots jauntily along; whilst bringing up the rear is a gem from the motoring world-a Triumph Mayflower-a real connoisseur's car. *J H Turner*

Sheffield Victoria, n.d: Although the wires are up, this is still very much a photograph rooted in the steam era. B1 No **61315**, a Darnall engine from 1948 to 1963, crosses the Wicker, passes No 3 signalbox and enters the station from the west with an Up express. Semaphores are still in use and the water column remains in evidence. Proof of the mix of old and new orders.

B.N.Collins

Sheffield Victoria, July 15th.1958: Aside from the obvious changes in motive power over the last three decades, the sheer lack of variety of modern coaching stock helps to make the modern scene that much less interesting than hitherto. A prime example of this is found in this splendid rolling stock study taken by Howard Turner a little over forty years ago. Howard had "just popped in" to Victoria in his lunch hour to see what was going on when he set upon this fine sight: a former Great Eastern Restaurant Car, No **E667E** in front in maroon livery, with an ex-GER open vehicle behind, both having just been detached from the "Boat Train", ex-Harwich. Crew members glance out from the second and third windows and coffee appears to be being poured from a silver plated pot. What would that fetch at Myers Grove today, one wonders?

J H Turner

Sheffield Victoria, September 6th 1894: A view looking north - east across from the east end of the station platforms towards the Effingham Street Gas Works. This was the grim, grey Sheffield of the Victorian era when life expectancy averaged a mere 40-odd years and a Sheffield cutlery grinder's was a quite a lot less. The centrepiece of our attention is Sacré class 12A 2-4-0 No **165**; the three occupants seem pre-occupied with matters below. Built in October 1885 as No. 545, this engine was re-numbered 165 in January 1894. It was withdrawn from service in April 1914 and scrapped in the June of that year.
Collection of J.Braithwaite

(Centre) Sheffield Victoria, n.d; A vintage scene alongside Sheffield No 2 signal box. Parker Class 6A1 0-6-0 No **552** poses, with enginemen, for the photographer. An MS&L cast iron fluted water column can be clearly seen for good measure. No 2 box controlled movements in and out of the north-west end of Bridgehouses Goods. The stone wall in the background is the same one seen in the picture of B1 No 61163. The terraced houses stand along Railway Street at its junction with Denholme Street. No 552 had been built in November 1887. The locomotive's stovepipe chimney was a Parker characteristic, but the double frames and smokebox wing-plates are a throwback to his predecessor, Sacré, features seen on his class 6A engine of 1874. Interestingly, the 6A1 Class were the first MS&L locomotives to be fitted with screw reversing gear. No.552 was fitted with a GCR No.1 standard boiler (with a Belpaire firebox) in January 1915. The engine was withdrawn in May 1928.
Collection of J.H.Turner

(Lower) Sheffield Victoria, May 4th 1929: D7 No **5691** runs towards the station with a Down express. The D7s (GCR 2/2A), like so many of the GCR 4-4-0 classes, had been conceived for express running over the London Extension. Long displaced now from their original territory, these handsome 4-4-0s served out their time on secondary duties over the width of their former parent system. No.5691 spent some time at Mexborough on workings from Doncaster to Penistone. And, indeed, the formation of the train, 6-wheeled MS&L stock, would suggest such a train.   *W.L.Good*

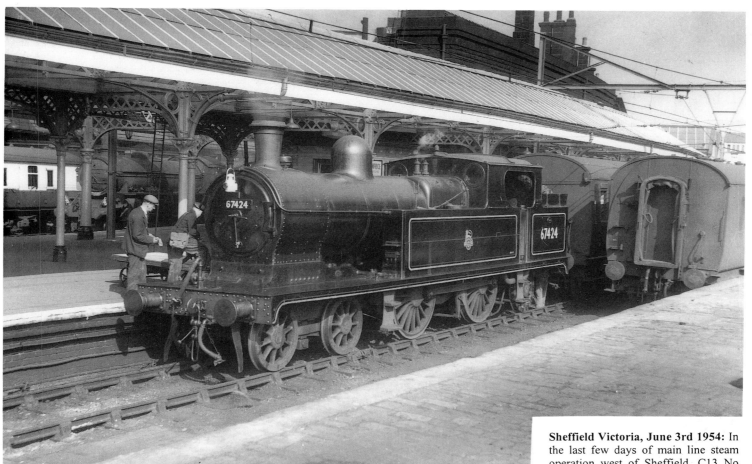

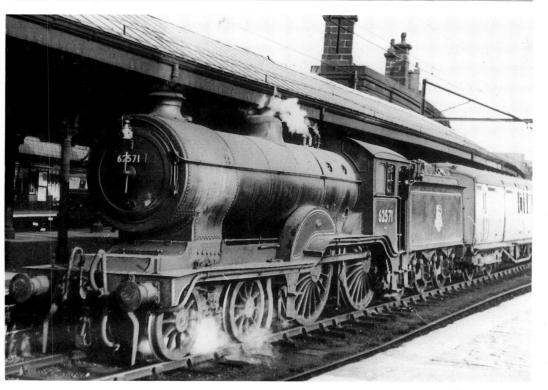

Sheffield Victoria, June 3rd 1954: In the last few days of main line steam operation west of Sheffield, C13 No **67424,** looking in spanking ex-works condition, simmers away in the bay at the west end of the station at the head of a stopping train to Penistone. The engine was then stationed at (39B) Darnall, the depot at that time being an out-station of Gorton (39A). Typical 1950s local journey over this line left Sheffield Victoria at 5.30 pm, called at Wadsley Bridge (5.39), Oughty Bridge (5.45) Deepcar for Stocksbridge (5.54) Wortley (5.57) and Penistone (6.05).

Ken Boulter

Sheffield Victoria, 1953: Former Great Eastern Railway 4-4-0s were, reportedly, rare sights at Victoria. This one, No **62571,** nestles in the bay with a Gresley brake 3rd behind the tender, possibly waiting for an incoming train. No 62571 began life in June 1909 as No 1820-one of the G E Class D56 7'-0" 4-4-0s, a type which began life in 1900 as the legendary Claud Hamilton engine. Under what must be one of the most complex rebuilding operations of any locomotive class, No 62571 eventually became re-classified as part of D16/3 in May, 1939. She was withdrawn in January 1959.

David Ibbotson

Sheffield Victoria, pre-WWI: Looking north west towards Bridgehouses and Neepsend, few pictures give a better example of the station's splendid ridge and furrow pattern of overall glass roof than this one. Twenty-five minutes past Noon sees Victoria bustling with human activity, but without a train in sight! Along platform 3, to the right of the picture, an elegant-looking lady appears to pause and gaze to her left; other passengers, both young and old, congregate over along the far platform. From here a sign directs passengers to "cross the line by the subway"- this thoroughfare having been opened in 1908, along with the formation of new platform roads. Notice the use of deep ash-ballasted trackwork, a hangover from Victorian practice.

Sheffield City Libraries

Sheffield Victoria, 1950s: A similar aspect to our Edwardian view, but this time looking east and gazing on a very different-looking station. Now in the era of the electrified railway the overall glass roof has gone, to be replaced by far less glamorous, but much more practical, structures. A grubby-looking K3, No **61838** gently sizzles as it backs down the centre road to take charge of a clutch of passenger stock. "What, Daddy,"a child of the future might ask, "were Telegrams?"   *J.H.Turner*

Sheffield Victoria, 1939: Two views of Up trains alongside platform 4 showing stark contrasts in express motive power in the period immediately prior to WWII. **(Above)** The old order. Great Central Atlantic No **5260**-at this time a Leicester engine and one of the last batch to be built, at Gorton in 1906-waits at the head of an express. Gresley coaching stock is in evidence, but it is not possible to discern the lettering on the coach roofboards. Notice the Fireman is "putting the bag in" by the gap in the roof awnings. Now long relegated to black livery, No 5260 was superheated in February 1935, but did not receive piston valve cylinders. She was withdrawn in December 1950. **(Below)** The Gresley era: An Immaculate Class V2 No **4828**, a Gorton engine in this period, and presenting an almost mystical sight in lined Apple green, blows off impatiently whilst awaiting departure. No 4828 was one of three V2s which had arrived at Gorton by 1939. Coach roofboard detail is not legible, but duties of the Gorton V2s at this time are known to have been the 8.20 pm Manchester London Road to Leicester with a return working of the Down Mail to Godley. Another working and, possibly, this is the one illustrated, was the 9.25 am Manchester to Hull express (which had set out from Liverpool at 8.30) as far as Sheffield. From here the V2 hauled the York to Bournemouth express (at 11.37), returning to Manchester at 2.28 pm on the 12.15 express from Marylebone.

both photographs; K.H.Boulter

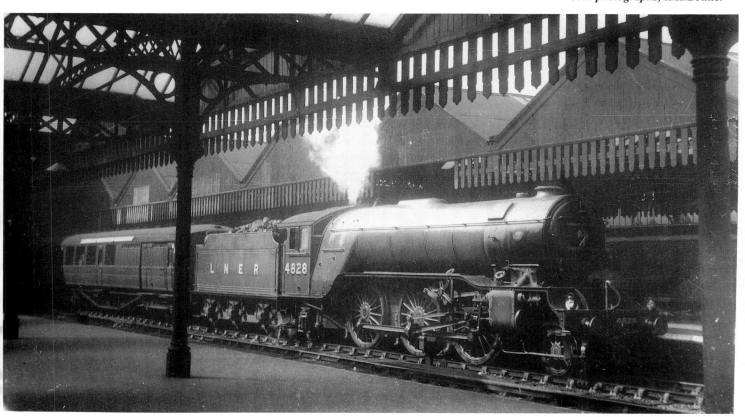

Sheffield Victoria, July 1967: Three o'clock on a summer afternoon sees the station almost twenty years into the era of British Railways. This was the sight that had greeted thousands of passengers over the years after the walk up the station approach road from its junction with Blonk Street and Furnival Road. Contemporary touches are provided by the sight of the Austin "black cab" taxi and the Ford Anglia (how many of us remember learning to drive in one of those vehicles?). Looking back on this sunny summer sight, it hardly seems possible that the station had less than three years of life left. *Sheffield City Libraries*

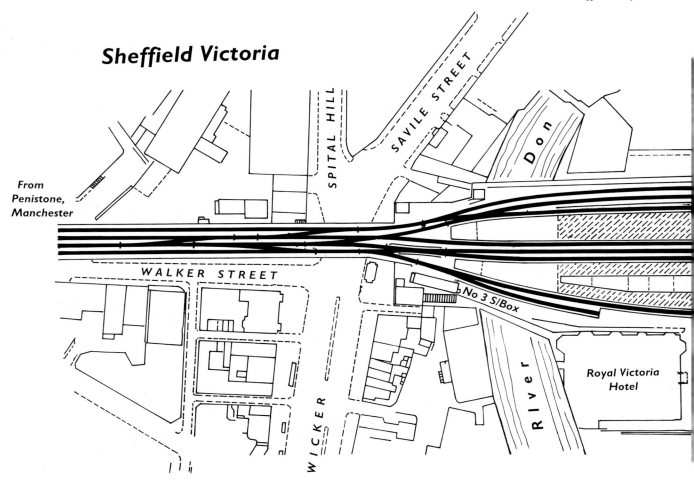

Sheffield Victoria

Sheffield Victoria, May 29th 1954: Brian Green, that foremost of Woodhead line photographers, managed to capture most points of the route on film prior to electrification. Pausing at Victoria on this fine May day, Brian found all roads occupied. Pride of place in the lens of his Ensign Selfix 82 camera was B17 No **61633** *Kimbolton Castle* (then a March engine). Seen alongside platform 4, the B17 has taken over the afternoon Liverpool (Central), via Manchester Central, to Harwich (Parkeston Quay) train. This was a post-War version of the famed "North Country Continental"-a complex through working from the north-west and the Midlands to the Great Eastern's port at Harwich.   *B.K.B.Green*

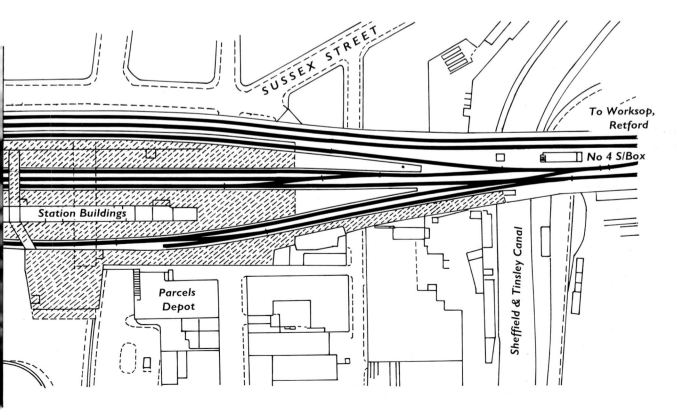

Wicker, c.1910: A delightful picture of the Wicker with part of the imposing main span of the viaduct showing behind the Sheffield Corporation tram No **37** picking up passengers for the Handsworth route. The very sturdy-looking Edwardian tram shelter is a thing of almost tram-like design itself! On its journey to Handsworth the No.37 will pass under the Great Central system once and over it twice and under the Midland Railway once; the two railways adding much of interest to the journey. Approaching is another tram, a No **87** which has come from Rotherham with whom Sheffield had a joint working arrangement, with Rotherham cars working into the city. Only cars from Rotherham showed the destination as "Sheffield", all other routes showing simply "City" with variations. Car No.37 was one of thirty-eight examples built by G.F.Milnes of Birkenhead in 1899-1900, originally open top and receiving a top cover in 1904. This car was sold in 1922 to the Gateshead & District Tramways Company. Car No.87, of similar design, was built by the Electric Railway & Tramway Carriage Company of Preston in 1900 and lasted in service until 1922. A similar car can be seen today at the National Tramway Museum in Crich, Derbyshire. The Wicker viaduct looks very blackened and has probably received no cleaning since its construction in 1848. Up above is a train of 6-wheeled compartment coaches forming a local which has almost certainly arrived from either Chesterfield or Retford. Notice the hoarding advertising the Empire Theatre, of several in Sheffield at this time. This particular theatre survived until the early 1960s. *Sheffield City Libraries*

"Old" Sheffield

Sheffield Victoria, c.1890s: Hatted ladies with long skirts, gentlemen with Top hats and rolled umbrellas and horse-drawn carriages of a bewildering variety: all could only point to the Victorian and Edwardian era when such things were a part of the everyday tapestry of human life. This was the Sheffield Victoria of the MS&LR and before the new station frontage, complete with clock tower, made its appearance in 1908. What delights were coming and going behind that frontage on this sunny day of long ago? *Sheffield City Libraries*

Sheffield Victoria, August 16th 1875: Britain was the most powerful nation on earth at this time-something reflected in the manner in which the reigning monarch and her immediate family were treated. Accordingly, no expense appears to have been spared in decorating the station for the visit of the Prince and Princess of Wales-the future King Edward VII and his wife, Alexandra. The clock shows Noon exactly and a beautifully polished Sacré 2-4-0 (Number unknown) bedecked with the Union Flag waits-possibly acting as a Pilot engine. Waiting officials and groups of police stand attentively around, whilst a lone figure-the Lord Mayor or Station-master-awaits in the centre of the platform, which appears to have been specially covered over. No expense seems to have been spared in decorating the building, even the roof trusses appear to have received treatment. An abundance of flags is hung-"The Stars and Stripes" appears too, whilst the number of leafy plants set around would do justice to a botanical garden! All this for a single visit; one can't help wondering how much notice the royal party took of it all.

Sheffield City Libraries

Sheffield Victoria, c.1920s: The much altered station frontage, a product of the re-modelling exercise undertaken by the GCR in 1908. Twelve minutes past four in the afternoon highlights the rather squat clock tower with flagpole atop, a diminutive structure and not at all like that at the station bearing the same name in Nottingham. To the right of the view can be seen the War Memorial erected by the Great Central in the aftermath of that most awful of conflicts and commemorating the 1,304 of the company's men who perished. Dedicated at a ceremony on August 9th 1922, the memorial was the scene for an annual Armistice Day service at which the centrepiece was the company's War Memorial engine, the legendary No 1165 *Valour*. In 1938 the memorial was re-sited inside the station as part of the re-modelling of the booking hall. Sadly, after Victoria's closure in 1970, the memorial was removed and re-sited ignominiously underneath the Wicker Arches where it remains out of sight, vandalised and all but forgotten. Surely, a city with such obvious Socialist proclivities should not have allowed this to happen? *Sheffield City Libraries*

Sheffield Victoria, c.1950: An almost eerie combination of light, dark and deep shadow dominate this platform scene as an unidentified A1 Pacific pulls away east with an Up express. Despite their predominance on the former Great Northern line, it should not be forgotten that A1 Pacifics had been regular performers on the Great Central main line from early in 1925. The Great Central bracket signals at the end of the platform would have dated from 1908/09 when new platforms and a new Down loop were brought into operation. Sheffield No.4 box can be seen in the distance, just beyond the engine.

Geoff Newall/courtesy Ted Hancock

Sheffield Victoria, July 15th 1958: The York to Bournemouth express has just arrived at the west end of platform 2 behind a rather begrimed B16/3 No **61464** of 50A, York. The York crew have just got off the locomotive, to be relieved by another set of men who will then take their charge to Darnall shed for disposal. The train left from the same platform just after 12 Noon, but of course, heading south behind another engine. Unfortunately, the number was not recorded on this occasion, but would probably have been a B1 or a V2. To the right is the high wall which separated the station from the path that ran alongside the Royal Victoria Hotel, giving access to both station and hotel from the Wicker lift and adjacent steps mentioned elsewhere. Sadly, today, only the hotel remains; its boundaries having been extended over recent years onto the site of the former station. **J.H.Turner**

Sheffield Victoria, Winter of 1957: Making a splendidly atmospheric start out of the station is B17 No **61643** *Champion Lodge*. This is another Harwich Boat Train shot; the Boat Train had left Liverpool at 12.50 pm, departure from Victoria being at 3.03 with arrival in Harwich at 8.41. No less than four engine changes were made on this cross-country journey. At Manchester Central (where the train reversed), Guide Bridge-where electric traction took over, then back to steam here at Sheffield and, finally at March-where No 61643 was stabled.   *J.H. Turner*

Sheffield Victoria, early 1950s: The days when "Spotters" wore well-polished shoes and belted raincoats help to date this picture. If you were the young man who was peering mischievously from behind the blue enamelled Sheffield Victoria sign, can you remember what your reaction was as you gazed upon B1 No **61004** *Oryx* coming into the station with a Down express. All the vintage touches from the pre-Group era: GCR-pattern semaphores, wooden bodied wagons, water column and industrial trappings in the form of tall chimneys, show the station and its environs as it had been for the best part of a century. A vintage view indeed.

Geoff Newall/Ted Hancock collection

Sheffield Victoria

Sheffield Victoria, n.d: Taken alongside one of the platform entrances, this notice is something that hardly requires a caption. Nothing, it seems, is new under the sun.

J.H.Turner

Sheffield Victoria, September 19th 1954: B12/3 No **61574** saunters into the station with two non-corridor coaches-by the looks of things to form part of an excursion working. Sheffield No 4 box can be seen in the background, the box's official name was "Sheffield East No 4", incidentally. Electrification is now in full swing-notice the newly-constructed brick cabin alongside the signalbox to house the myriad of relays and other electrical apparatus which were part of the re-signalled layout here. No 61574 was one of the ten LNER B12s built by Beyer,Peacock & Co. in 1928. My teenage "Spotting" records show just eleven B12s seen. Alas, this was not one of them. No 61574 was missing from my treasured summer 1957 Ian Allan "Combined", the engine, then based at Grantham, having been condemned in January of that year.

A.G.Ellis

Sheffield Victoria, May 19th 1948: A complete contrast to the later view showing the B12. Here, just over four months into the era of British Railways, is the Victoria of the steam era, with semaphore signals-even one or two GC ones-and a locomotive still carrying its LNER insignia. J11 No **4360** runs past No.4 signalbox in the direction of Darnall. The photographer noted that a yellow fog was hanging around the station when he took this picture.

P.M.Alexander

Sheffield Victoria, c.1950: We referred in the Penistone section to the "South Yorkshireman", a true BR era named train which connected the famous northern woollen town of Bradford with the Capital via GC metals. In a scene devoid of any electrification paraphernalia, B1 No **61182** presents a splendid sight as she pulls strongly away south with the Up working of this famous train. The time will be about 11.27 am and the B1 will have taken over here from an ex-LMS "Black Five." Calling at Nottingham, Loughborough, Leicester, Rugby and Aylesbury (a stop added later on)-arrival in Marylebone was at 3.30pm. Cecil.J.Allen, that most experienced of writers on train working, recorded in his "Titled Trains of Great Britain" in 1953 that the LMS Black Five that had brought the "South Yorkshireman" into Sheffield worked south as far as Leicester with the following York to Bournemouth train. The same engine then returned with the northbound Bournemouth to York as far as Sheffield. From here it returned to Bradford with the Down "South Yorkshireman." The small cluster of ex-GCR signals on the left-hand side will be familiar by now. Notice the new colour light installation due to replace the LNER standard upper quadrant signal. Complete with "theatre-type" route indicator, the signals have been turned away from the direction of traffic pending their commissioning. *N.E.Stead collection*

Sheffield Victoria, September 14th 1929: D49s were not the most photographed engines in this neck of the woods, so it was quite a treat to have discovered this splendid shot taken by W.Leslie Good showing D49/1 No **253** *Oxfordshire* standing in the station with an Up express. No 253 belonged to York shed at this time, so the possibility is that the train could be a York or Newcastle train to Bournemouth via Banbury. *Oxfordshire* was taken off at Sheffield and, although the substitute engine was not recorded, the possibility is that a GC Atlantic or one of the two original GC 6'-9" 4-6-0s took the train south. The GCR ran a Restaurant Corridor Express from York to Bournemouth. In 1922, the last year of the company's existence, the through train left York at 10.13am and Sheffield at 10.45; arrival in Bournemouth was at 6.13pm. The photographer is well "off limits" here, presenting us with an aspect of the station rarely seen. Glancing back towards the station, notice the presence of the overall roof-still largely intact, and the signal gantry spread across the tracks. Part of the Effingham Street Gasworks can be made out over on the far right-hand side. *W.L.Good*

Sheffield Victoria, September 14th 1929: W.Leslie Good had a field day at Victoria on this early autumn day. Accompanied by fellow RCTS member H.J.Stretton-Ward, Good can only be envied for the wonderful assortment of former GCR motive power that was on offer that day to be viewed through the lens of his camera. Fortunately, his legacy is reasonably well preserved and thanks to the good offices and darkroom skills of Gordon Coltas we can gaze on two more examples of his work. **(Above)** A "Sam" 4-6-0 No **5425** *City of Manchester*, then stationed at Neepsend and still in lined LNER green, waits to leave east-bound with an express-possibly bound for Cleethorpes or Hull. Flanking the train are a C2, (ex-GN small Atlantic) No **3254** and a "Pom-Pom" No **5197** on the right-hand side. **(Below)** The Lancashire, Derbyshire & East Coast Railway had been incorporated into the MS&L from August 5th 1891. Always a Tank Engine company, the LDEC relied on contractors for its locomotives. No **6402** was a product of Kitson & Co., having been built in December 1898. Seen at the east end of Victoria, No 6402 was on station pilot duty at the time. An interesting-looking former GCR clerestory coach can be seen behind the engine. A D9, number not known, can be glimpsed off to the far left-hand side.   *W.Leslie Good*

Sheffield Victoria, August 23rd 1952: What more splendid sight could there be, in modern times at any rate, than the sight of one of Gresley's magnificent Pacifics striking away with an express? We commented earlier on the incidence of LNER Pacifics on former GC tracks; here, by a master photographer, the late lamented Tom Lewis, is a splendid study. A3 No **60054** *Prince of Wales* (née *Manna*) pulls away from platform 4 with the 8.25am express from Manchester London Road to Marylebone. *Prince of Wales* was rebuilt from an A1 in 1943; notice, though, that she still carries right-hand drive. A B1 simmers in the centre road, but no doubt the onlookers on the opposite platform are having their attention diverted by the thunderous sound emitted by No **60054.** Possibly recognising the photographer, the driver looks immensely pleased at having been caught on camera. For posterity let me pass on Tom Lewis's exposure notes: Exposure 1/250 at f11; material was HP3 plate (Tom's favourite material) and developer was Johnson's Fine Grain.

Tom Lewis

Sheffield Victoria

Sheffield Victoria, n.d: Class B8 (former GCR Class 1A) No **5446** *Earl Roberts of Kandahar* waits alongside platform 4 with an Up stopping train. This picture, though of slightly indifferent technical quality, shows well a member of this ex-GC mixed traffic engine in LNER days. Despite widespread collection and research, this has been the only image I could manage to find showing a Glenalmond at work in the Sheffield area. **Author's collection**

Robinson's first passenger engine for the GCR, the 11B 4-4-0 ultimately became classed as LNER D9. The class was in ample profusion at Sheffield Victoria in the 1920s and 30s as these last views show.

(Above) Sheffield Victoria, early 1930s: Giving a good overall view of the east end of the station, No **6017** departs with an Up stopping train. This slightly panoramic view shows well the overall station roof, the Royal Victoria Hotel and something of the industry which surrounded the railway here at this time. In the right background the Effingham Street gas works and commented on earlier stands across from the chimneys of the Sheaf Steel and Iron works which was spread-eagled under the railway in front of Sussex Street and between the Sheffield & South Yorkshire Navigation, Blast Lane and Lumley Street. In the middle foreground can be seen the goods line, added as part of the enlargement of the station in the early years of the century. The tracks immediately in front of the photographer led down to the former GCR's Park Station Coal and Lime depot at Blast lane. This was served by a canal wharf and basin near to the junction of Navigation Hill and Blast Lane itself.   *Courtesy of Roger Carpenter*

(Below) Sheffield Victoria, 1939: Carrying express lights, No **5105** backs down alongside platform 4 to collect its train. Although in the rather funereal black livery, the engine appears to be well-polished and quite gleams in the sunlight. Compatriot No **6022** sits in the back platform; it will be noticed that this engine has the earlier livery style which retained the brass beading causing the rather awkward placing of the cabside numerals. No 5105 had been allocated to Mexborough from 1936 and the likelihood is that the engine is taking over a working to Cleethorpes.   *Ken Boulter*

Darnall Shed, April 4th 1959: A well-detailed panorama of the shed, but one presenting ominous signs of things to come with two long rows of locomotives stored "out of use." Altogether, seventeen locomotives were slumbering amongst the huge mounds of coal, although in the photograph only fifteen can be seen. The most notable are four D11 "Directors" of which No **62664** *Princess Mary* and No **62668** *Jutland* can be identified; in the distance are No **62667** *Somme* and No **62670** *Marne*. The rest of the group consisted of three K2s, Nos **61728/47/61**, the latter having only recently arrived back from Cowlairs works in Glasgow after a heavy repair and a full repaint in lined black livery. This particular K2, No.61728, did little work afterwards and, towards the end of its existence, was transferred to King's Cross shed for stationary boiler duty. The other locomotives in the scene were five J39s, Nos **64719/46** and Nos **64804/08/78** and, finally, five N5s, Nos **69258/86/90/94** and No **69314**. Despite the forlorn sight, the "Directors" and the K2s were returned to traffic to cover Summer work in both 1959 and 1960, but it is doubtful if the J39s and N5s saw any further use. Apart from the stored locomotives, the shed is well occupied with a number of engines in steam. In the background is the turntable, Electric and DMU repair shed, coaling tower and, beyond, the huge complex of Messrs. Cravens Carriage & Wagon Works, who were at this time building Diesel railcars for British Railways. Darnall soldiered on for a few more years with the steam allocation gradually giving way to Diesels. Sadly, closure finally came in 1963 after a short life of only some 20 years. Today, there is nothing left here, the whole site having been completely cleared in the last year or so.

J.H.Turner

Darnall Shed

Darnall locomotive depot was sited some two miles east of Sheffield Victoria on the GCR's main line. Beyond Darnall, via Handsworth, the line diverged at Woodhouse Junction, the former MSLR route continuing via Worksop and Retford and the London Extension going due south via Beighton and Chesterfield. Darnall has its own station, opened in 1849; a north to east connecting curve, opened in 1873, enabled coal traffic from the South Yorkshire coalfield to eastern stations and ports to avoid Sheffield. The curve formed a triangle from Attercliffe Junction down to Darnall Junction. Woodburn Junction, on the triangle's western flank, controlled the entry and exit to Darnall Loco from the Sheffield side, the former being accessed via a newly-built flyover crossing the main line.

As mentioned earlier, conditions at Neepsend shed had bordered on the intolerable for many years. The LNER chose the site at Darnall in 1936. Ample spare land was available and easy access to Sheffield Victoria was to hand. The depot opened its doors to traffic in April 1943. Little in the way of an announcement was made, conditions of wartime secrecy pertaining. An illustration in a contemporary magazine showed a new locomotive depot "somewhere in the North Midlands." The depot, large by any standards, had a staff of 750. The main running shed consisted of ten through roads covered by a "westernlight"roof-essentially a series of sawtooth gables. New messrooms were provided, along with a kitchen and a fifty-bed dormitory. A 70ft. turntable and wet ashpits 200ft. long completed the facilities. Darnall, ultimately, housed electric locomotives as well. Whether this was foreseen when the LNER constructed the depot is a moot point. One report suggests that a four-road shed was planned for electric traction; in the event, only accommodation for two roads was built; this was opened in 1954. On this side of the Pennines, electric stabling was also available at Wath and Rotherwood, east of Darnall and the limit of the MSW electrification. Darnall depot had only a short life. The shed was coded 39B and was classed as an outstation of Gorton at one time. Under later re-organisation, Darnall was coded 41A. Closure to steam was effected on June 17th 1963; complete closure came just over two years later, on Monday, October 4th 1965.

Darnall Shed, Repair Shop, c.1954: A fully covered repair shop complete with electric lighting and heating was a rare bird indeed in the days of steam locomotive maintenance. No date has been recorded for this picture but, no doubt, one of my more avid readers will be scouring his Loco Shed books to tell me! O4/8 No **63882** stands over to the left of the shop; her rods have been dropped so re-metalling of the bushes is probably in progress. From another locomotive, one set of coupled wheels is seen awaiting attention. In the background B1 No **61152** is similarly stripped, her left-hand front cylinder cover having been removed. A J39, to the left, completes the trio. It is perhaps through scenes like this that we are reminded, as mere enthusiasts, of the vast amount of heavy manual work that had to be expended by shed staff to keep the wheels of their motive power turning.
G.Newall/Ted Hancock collection

Darnall M.P.D, n.d: Sentinel Class Y3 0-4-0 No **8176** standing alongside the shed. The still new construction shows something of the showpiece construction of the depot, something that was light years removed from a great many steam sheds.   *B.N.Collins*

(Right) Darnall Shed, April 30th 1950: A splendid study of O4/7 No **63661** standing cold, but quite immaculate, outside the shed. The early shed code of 39B is carried on the smokebox. A Class B1 loco', still carrying evidence of its LNER parentage, is seen alongside. Notice the troughing over the shed entrance to convey smoke through the roof ducts. The corrugated steel roofing is sure evidence of wartime building provision. ***Author's collection***

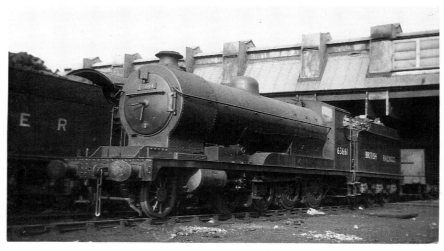

(Left) Darnall Loco, n.d: B1 No **61087** was one of one hundred engines built by North British Locomotive Co. over a twelve month period from April 1947. She was allocated to Doncaster when this picture was taken-out of steam and with heavy lime deposits oozing from a boiler washout plug. A young man has climbed into the cab and poses for the camera in the fireman's seat. Who was he? A visitor, an engine cleaner with aspirations to move on to the footplate, or a fitter who happened to be working on the engine? Does anyone recognise him today? No 61087 was condemned on December 5th 1965. She was sold for scrap to Garnham, Harris and Elton of Chesterfield. ***J.H.Turner***

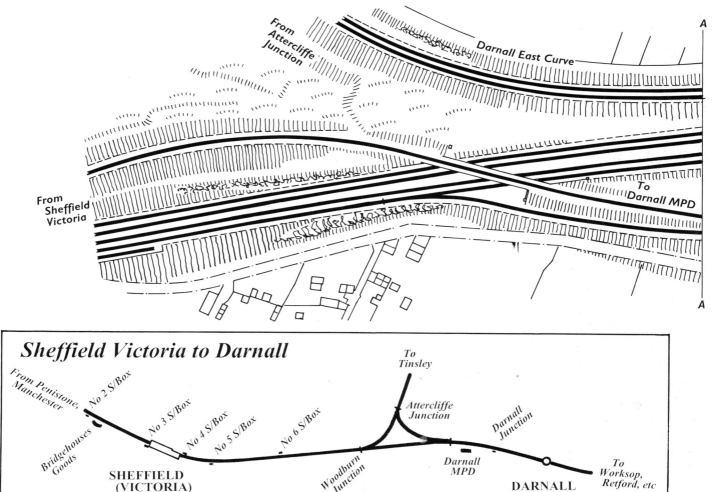

Darnall M.P.D, n.d: The intrepid photographer has scaled the coaling tower to provide us with this and the view opposite. **(Above)** The "westernlight" roof of the shed is shown to advantage here with its numerous ventilation ducts. This view looks west; faintly visible through the middle foreground is the western-side entrance road that crossed the main line via a flyover from Woodburn Junction. It is just possible to make this out to the left of the OHL structures on the right-hand side. The 70 ft. turntable makes an obvious presence in the middle of the view. The two-road electric shed stood off to the right at the bottom of the newly laid roadway.

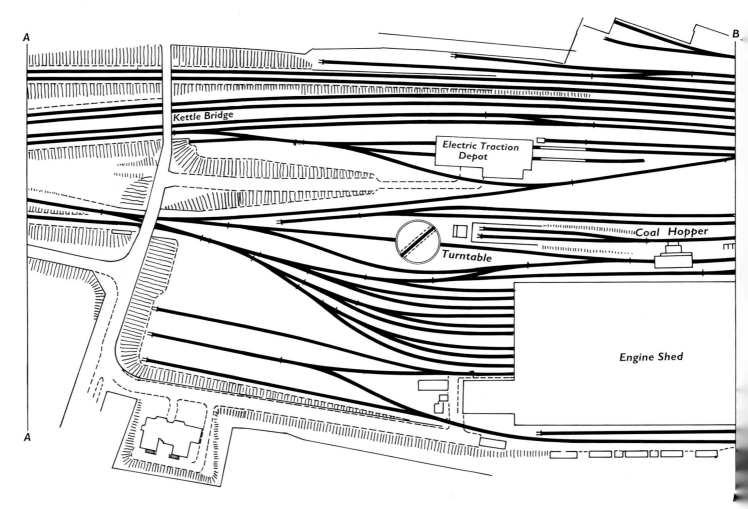

(This page) Turning around, the main line is on the left-hand side and we are looking towards Darnall Station and Handsworth. Spread over the foreground is a good assortment of motive power: a J39, "Austerity" 2-8-0, O4, B1, K2, and a J11 all being noted. The long building in the background, standing at right-angles to the main line, belonged to the Sheffield Wire Rope Co.Ltd., one of the many factories in the city suburbs that handled products of the steel industry. Darnall Junction box-seen on the extreme left-controlled movements to and from this end of the shed and the main line.

Both pictures: G.Newall/Ted Hancock collection

B

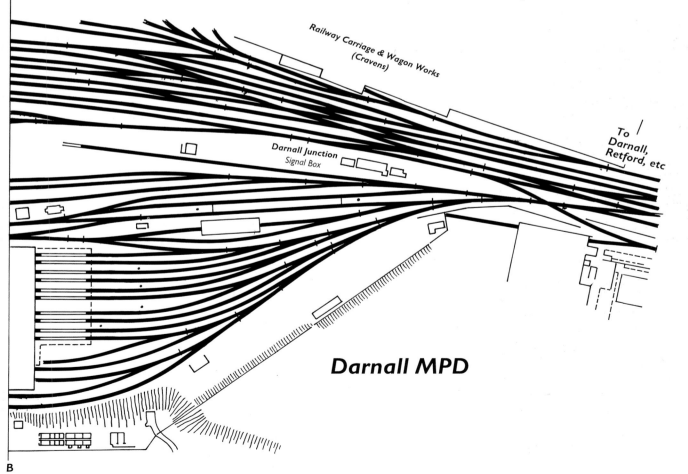

Railway Carriage & Wagon Works
(Cravens)

Darnall Junction
Signal Box

To
Darnall,
Retford, etc

Darnall MPD

B

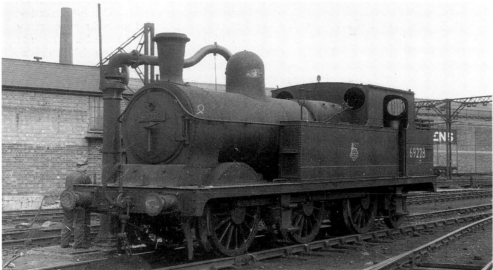

Here we have a chance to observe some former MS&L and GCR engine types that were working their days out at Darnall in the early years of British Railways.

Darnall Shed, June 13th 1948: Former GC Atlantic No **2918** began life as No 260 of Class 8B and was the first of eight 4-4-2s built at Gorton in 1906. No.2918 was allocated to Lincoln when this picture was taken and would have been working stopping passenger and some goods trains between there and Sheffield. A couple of details are worthy of note: The engine has twin handles to the smokebox door in place of the single GC pattern with handwheel; 2918 is superheated and is fitted with sight feed lubrication-notice the feed pipes along the side; this particular member was one of seven (of what became C4/2 Atlantics) to retain slide valves. No.2918 had the distinction of being the last Great Central Atlantic to be withdrawn-in December 1950. She was cut up at Gorton.

H.C.Casserley

Darnall Shed Yard, September 6th 1953: Class N4 0-6-2 tank No **69228** fills its tanks with water at the top of the yard; Darnall Junction signalbox is seen behind. The works of Messrs Cravens, a concern well known in Sheffield for both road and rail vehicles can be seen across the main line. N4s were not often seen on passenger duty in the city; but, in their long lives, they worked pretty well the whole gamut of freight and shunting operations at sites both in and outside the Sheffield boundaries. Examples would have included empty stock movements in and out of Victoria, shunting duties at Bridgehouses and work at Park and Blast Lane sidings as well as duties out at Penistone-shunting at Barnsley Junction, for example. No.69228 appeared on the MS&L in 1890, a product of Neilson & Co. She was withdrawn in December 1954.

H.F.Wheeler/Roger Carpenter collection

Darnall Shed, April 1947: The Robinson Directors were superb engines and deserve to be ranked among the best of the British 4-4-0 types. Carrying the number **2657**, the short-lived 1946 assignation, Class D10 *Sir Berkeley Sheffield* looks grimy and bedraggled as it stands in steam and blowing off alongside N4 tank No **9232**. All the original Directors (D10s) had been concentrated at Sheffield during WWII where they worked north to York, west to Manchester and south to Leicester. It is worth noting that their work over Woodhead was often with the heavily loaded 10 or 11 coach 5.30pm train from Sheffield. *Sir Berkeley Sheffield* was sent west to Northwich, on the CLC, in the latter part of 1947 where it earned its keep on stopping trains from Chester to Manchester Central. It was withdrawn from Northwich in March 1953.   *R.K.Blencowe collection*

Darnall M.P.D; June 1955: Clouds bask in the summer sky over eastern Sheffield, the shed is packed with locomotives, but none are in steam and nothing moves. This was a dark time for Darnall and, indeed, for the British Railway system as a whole. At midnight on May 28th 1955, members of ASLEF began a ruinous strike, the first official railway withdrawal of labour for almost 30 years. ASLEF called the strike to secure for footplatemen the pay differentials that the union saw as legitimate for the skill and responsibility involved in the work of their members. The strike lasted for seventeen days and produced a great deal of inter-union hostility (the NUR had ordered their enginemen to work normally).Though the recommendations of an independent arbitrator (Lord Justice Morris) appointed by the Government did result in some small gains, the railways lost an estimated £10M worth of receipts and some traffic was lost to the railways, never to return. We can take advantage of this view of the depot to look at the water tank towering above the shed roof. Holding 100,000 gallons, the tank, somewhat unusually, was disguised by a pitched roof.

B.N.Collins

Darnall Station, c.1958: Darnall Station stands some thirty chains from the site of the now long-closed locomotive depot and 2 miles from Sheffield Victoria. Opened as Darnal on February 12th 1849 by the then Sheffield & Lincolnshire Junction Railway, the station had become known as Darnall by 1877. The name Darnall for Handsworth appears in the 1910 timetables and this continued until around 1950. By 1955, however, plain Darnall was in vogue-this name appearing here on the blue enamelled signboard. The single island platform is nicely decorated with neatly walled flower beds. MS&L influence is detected, once again, in the shape of the lamp posts. Here we are looking east towards Orgreaves and Woodhouse Junction; houses on Kirby Road and Station Road can be seen to the left. 9F 2-10-0 No **92193** simmers away over on the Down Goods line.

W.A.Camwell

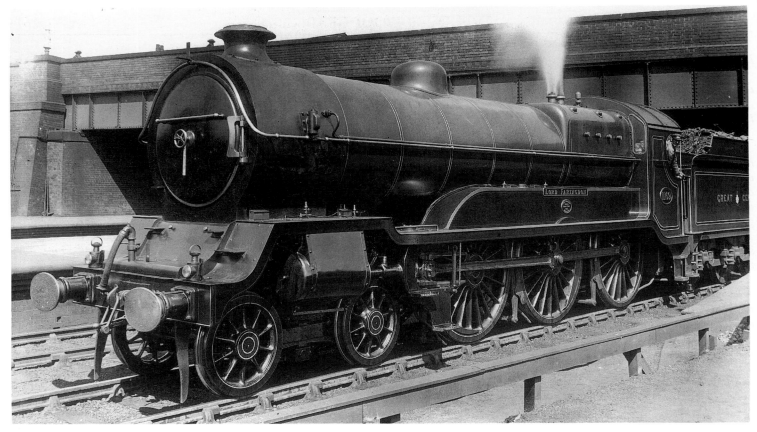

A Trip Over Woodhead -1920

  The respected locomotive engineer E. C. Poultney O.B.E. wrote a fine series of articles in "The Engineer" magazine after the First War. Entitled "Locomotive Footplate Experiences", Poultney combined expert knowledge of the locomotive with a fine brush journalistic style. Few modern-day enthusiasts will have read these articles which made me feel that this particular gem was a "must" for this volume. The published description covered the whole run from Manchester to Marylebone and gives an excellent contemporary account of what was then Robinson's flagship locomotive-the 9P 4-6-0. Reproduced here is that part of Poultney's journey just beyond Sheffield to Staveley. Readers may like to know that the description of the entire trip appeared in "The Engineer" for April 8th 1921.

  "The line between Manchester and Leicester presents several difficulties so far as gradients are concerned. To begin with, there is the long pull up to Woodhead, and through the tunnel to a point a quarter of a mile on the Manchester side of Dunford Bridge, 22.3 miles from London Road; then follows a stretch of 18.9 miles downhill to Sheffield. From Sheffield to Staveley is also for most part downhill except for the first 2½ miles, which are on rising gradients. Between Staveley and Pilsley the 8 miles are all uphill, and then the line falls almost all the way to Nottingham, 79.4 miles from Manchester, and 26.1 miles from Pilsley. The 23.3 miles between Nottingham and Leicester are generally on upward inclines. Analysing the road more closely, there are for the first 5 miles from London Road up to Guide Bridge 2½ miles of 1 in 176 to 1 in 100, and about 1½ miles of 1 in 133 and 1 in 364, and about ¼ mile of level on which the station is situated. From Guide Bridge to Woodhead, 19.1 miles, the chief gradients begin with a short length of 1 in 97, followed successively by 1 in 143, 2 miles; 1 in 122, 1½ miles; 1 in 100, 2¼ miles; and 5 miles of 1 in 117 to Woodhead. From Woodhead to

Dunford Bridge, 3.2 miles, 2¾ miles of which are in tunnel, are, with the exception of the last ¼ mile before reaching Dunford Bridge, on a rising gradient of 1 in 201. The principal falling gradients from the summit to Sheffield are 2½ miles of 1 in 135, 5 miles varying from 1 in 124 to 1 in 100, followed by about 11 miles on most of which the line falls at 1 in 120 and 1 in 132, Sheffield Station itself being on a level section about three-quarters of a mile in length. Leaving Sheffield the line rises for about 1 mile at the rate of 1 in 144, followed by 1 in 320 and 1 in 156; then come 4 miles at 1 in 150 up and 1 in 137 down, with a short compensated stretch to Staveley. From Staveley to Pilsley there is a long bank of 1 in 100 up for almost 4 miles, followed by short gradients of 1 in 100 to 1 in 264, & c., and then for 17.9 miles the line generally ascends to Nottingham, the chief descents being at rates of 1 in 132, 1 in 660, and 1 in 130. From Nottingham to Leicester the line generally rises, the chief up gradients being at the rate of 1 in 176, with short lengths of of 1 in 330 and 1 in 264. Between these points there are also downhill stretches, so that although Leicester lies somewhat higher than Nottingham, the 23.3 miles between these stations are not really difficult to run, even with a heavy train.

  For my journey over the Great Central, I decided upon the 2.15 p.m. ex London Road to Marylebone restaurant car express, which is due in London at 7.00 p.m., and reaches Leicester, 102.7 miles, at 4.51. Between Manchester and Leicester this train stops at Guide Bridge, 5 miles, Penistone, 28.3 miles, Sheffield, 41.3 miles, and at Nottingham, 79.4 miles. From

Manchester to Leicester the train consisted of nine large eight-wheeled coaches, the total weight of which was 312 tons, no allowance being made for passengers and baggage. I may mention that as far as Nottingham the train was very well filled, and on inquiring the reason, I learnt that a number of passengers were going to Nottingham to attend the Goose Fair.

I specially requested Mr. Robinson to let me have one of his four-cylinder express engines for the first part of my journey and it was arranged that No. 1169, "Lord Faringdon", the first engine of the series, and built at Gorton in 1917, should be put on the train. This engine had been in service three years, and was just going into the shops for her first general repairs after running 120,000 miles, but was kept out to make one more journey specially on my account, though I believe the works manager had the pit ready for her in the shops.

In general design the engines of this class resemble the 4-6-0 locomotives of the "Sir Sam Fay" class but they differ in one important particular, and that is, they have, instead of two inside cylinders, four cylinders. They are arranged in line across the engine, two inside, under the smoke-box, and two outside. The inside motion drives the leading coupled wheels, and the outside motion drives the second or centre coupled axle. The inside cranks are placed at an angle of 90 deg. to each other, and adjacent inside and outside cranks on each side of the engine are opposite to each other. Two sets of ordinary link motion operate the four piston valves, which are placed on top of their respective cylinders. The link motion is connected to the valve spindles by means of rockers, and the arrangement is such that each of the two adjacent valves on the right and left of the engine respectively move in the same direction. the inside valves have inside admission, and the outside valves have outside admission, and in this way the two sets of valve gear work the four valves, one set for two adjacent cylinders, the pistons of which travel in opposite directions. In order to keep the outside connecting-rods of substantially the same length and, incidentally, the same weight, as those for the inside cylinders, the outside piston-rods are made much longer than usual, which arrangement, combined with the relatively short connecting-rods, has necessitated placing the slide bars further back and also providing means for supporting the long piston-rods. This object is gained by using a steel casting in outside contour something like an elongated horseshoe magnet. The inside of the legs are of course parallel and are fitted with machined fitting strips on which the slide bars are bolted. The connecting-rods work through the open ends of the legs of this casting, and at the closed end is a cylindrical piece, bored and bushed which carries the piston-rod. The piston valves used on this and other Great Central engines are of a special design known as a combined piston and pressure release valve. They permit the release of any undue pressure in the cylinders and provide for the circulation of air from one side of the pistons to the other when the engine is coasting. The footplate fittings are very well arranged, and comprise one or two special features. One is a novel type of lubricator, known as an "Intensifore" lubricator. It is really nothing more or less than a hydraulic intensifier, in which steam acts on a piston through the medium of water, the condensate of the steam to some extent. The under or reverse side of this piston is in the oil chamber, so that on steam being turned on pressure is put on the oil, which is then, by means of pipes, taken where required. Distributors fitted with sight feed glasses

are mounted on each side panel of the cab, from whence pipes are led to the cylinders and valve chests and also to the driving axle-boxes. Another special device is an arrangement working in conjunction with the regulator handle. This is a header discharge valve; the valve itself is mounted on the left-hand side of the smoke-box, its function being to open when the regulator is shut, and thus to establish connection between the superheated steam side of the header and the blast pipe; by this means all steam in the superheater is immediately discharged after the regulator is closed. A blower valve of special design is also used. This valve will either operate the blower only, or at the same time govern a supply of steam to the elements. When on closing the regulator the blower is started, which is always the case, this valve is turned to the left, thus giving steam to the blower and at the same time allowing steam to flow through the elements; this circulating steam also finds its way to the valves and pistons and acts as a lubricating medium when the locomotive is running with steam shut off. The Great Central uses a screw reverse gear, which, together with the vacuum brake ejector and the steam brake valve that works in conjunction with it, is arranged on the driver's side of the footplate, which is on the right hand. Sanding gear of the ordinary gravity type is used, and is fitted to the leading and centre coupled wheels for forward running, and to the trailing wheels for back gear running. The fire-door is something like a butterfly valve, very similar to the arrangement used on the Great Northern. It is placed somewhat higher from the engine deck than is usual, but the fireman seemed, nevertheless, to do his work quite easily.

The cab is, like most of those in use on the railways of this country, much superior to those employed formerly. The canopy is carried back over the footplate, and is supported by turned pillars. The windows are at the sides of the front plate, being shaped at the top to flow the curve of the roof and the top corners of the Belpaire fire-box. Generally, a good view ahead is possible. In fact, as it seems to me, it does not appear to matter much if the driver is on the same side as the signals or not, or where the windows are placed in the specactle plate; that is to say, more or less over the boiler as they used to be, or at the sides, as even now with the much larger boilers used, the driver can as a rule see his signals. If semaphores are well placed, and on posts of sufficient height, having regard to their background, there is with very few exceptions no difficulty in sighting them. The all-important thing is to have them properly placed.

We made a very punctual start at 2.15pm., and, as is usual, the fireman began to put coal on immediately. The left-hand injector was also started. The steam pressure was about 175 lb., and between London Road and Guide Bridge the regulator was half open, and the reverse gear in notch 3½ from the centre, equivalent to about 53 per cent cut-off. The 5 miles up to Guide Bridge took exactly 10 min., the arrival time being 2.25, and we left again at 2.26 for the long pull up to Dunford Bridge. The 14.15 miles up to Woodhead, passed at 2.51½, were covered in 26½ min., against 27 min.allowed. For the whole distance the regulator was half open, and the gear in notch 3½, 53 per cent. cut-off, and the steam pressure was never below 170 lb., and generally above 175 lb. Firing was naturally rather frequent, about ten or twelve shovels of coal every 2 to 2¼ min.

A few miles byond Guide Bridge the weather conditions changed considerably, for at starting from London Road the sun shone quite brightly, and it was a fine autumn day, but as we got higher and higher we ran into what were really the clouds, which were settling down over the mountain tops in the distance, and the weather became thick, and with it very damp, at Woodhead the fog being fairly dense. The average speed between Guide Bridge and Woodhead was 32 miles per hour, and the 3.2 miles bewteen Woodhead and Dunford Bridge, nearly the whole distance being in the single-line tunnel, took 5½ min., Dunford Bridge being passed at 2.57. During almost the whole of the time we were in the tunnel, the fireman worked the sanding gear and the driver held the regulator ready to shut off if the engine slipped, which, however, it never did. Once in the tunnel a little coal was put on, but only about five shovels full. At Woodhead the steam pressure was 180 lb., and on passing Dunford Bridge the gauge showed 150 lb.

The distance between Dunford Bridge and Penistone is 6 miles, and we stopped in Penistone Station at 3.4½, or half a minute late, the distance having been run in 7½ min., equal to 48 miles per hour. The fog here was much thicker than at Woodhead, and going down the bank, each time we approached a distant signal the driver always made an application of the continuous brake, thus slowing the train slightly until he assured himself that the arm was off, and that is why the time between passing Woodhead and stopping at Penistone was one minute longer than the booked allowance of 12 min. At Penistone the weather was rather thick, with a fine rain falling, and owing to the large number of passengers about we were 2 min. 55 sec. late in leaving, not getting away till 3.9 and 55 sec., instead of 3.7. The 12.9 miles down to Sheffield took 16 min. 55 sec., against the 17 min. Allowed, the arrival time being 32.6 and 50 sec. This must be considered good work, as all the way down the brakes were frequently applied, until we were quite certain of the signals. Driver Chapman handled the engine very well down the steep bank, and the way in which he operated it interested me greatly. At Sheffield the tender tank was replenished with water, and

Chapman and I looked round the engine to see if everything was cool, and found all the journals and big ends in good condition. Driver Chapman, it may be of interest to note, is one of Mr. Robinson's best known enginemen, and enjoyed the friendship of your celebrated correspondent, the late C. Rous Marten, who rode with him on several occasions.

We left Sheffield after a wait of 2 min. 55 sec. at 3.29¾, three-quarters of a minute late. Owing to the weather conditions, the rails here were very greasy, making it almost as difficult to start without opening the sand valves as without opening the regulator. The regulator was first of all one third open, and then later half open, while the engine was almost in full gear getting the train into speed going up the 1 in 144 gradient out of the station. The pressure meanwhile fell back from 180 lb. to 170 lb., but later on the gear being notched up, quickly moved up nearby to the 180 mark. The 20.2 miles between Sheffield and Pilsley, passed at 4.0 and 25 sec., took 30 min. 40 sec. Most of the distance is uphill, the last 8 miles being continuously so at rates of 1 in 100, 1 in 115, and 1 in 300, &c. The average speed for this section was 39.8 miles per hour.

AUTHOR'S FOOTNOTE: Perusal of the GCR locomotive shopping records prove Poultney wrong in his statement that Robinson kept No 1169 back from shopping especially for his run. Assuming Poultney made his journey some time around October 1920, No 1169 was then just a fraction under three years old. She had already had one General Repair-from 8/03/19 to 12/04/19 and had clocked up 72,885 miles. On 16/10/20, after running a further 75,010 miles, the engine entered Gorton Works for a second General Repair-not the first as stated. The recorded mileage at this point in the engine's life was almost 149,000, well over the 120,000 stated in the article. She was in shops until 11/12/20. Just to complete this little pen picture; *Lord Faringdon* had 1,104,465 miles recorded to his credit when the engine was condemned on December 6th 1947.